Skillet
SENSATIONS

RDA ENTHUSIAST BRANDS, LLC
MILWAUKEE, WI

Skillet
SENSATIONS

EDITORIAL
EDITOR-IN-CHIEF Catherine Cassidy
VICE PRESIDENT, CONTENT OPERATIONS Kerri Balliet
CREATIVE DIRECTOR Howard Greenberg

MANAGING EDITOR/PRINT & DIGITAL BOOKS Mark Hagen
ASSOCIATE CREATIVE DIRECTOR Edwin Robles Jr.

ASSOCIATE EDITOR Molly Jasinski
LAYOUT DESIGNER Courtney Lovetere
EDITORIAL PRODUCTION MANAGER Dena Ahlers
EDITORIAL PRODUCTION COORDINATOR Jill Banks
COPY CHIEF Deb Warlaumont Mulvey
COPY EDITOR Chris McLaughlin
CONTRIBUTING COPY EDITOR Kristin Sutter

FOOD EDITORS Gina Nistico; James Schend;
Peggy Woodward, RDN
RECIPE EDITORS Sue Ryon (lead); Mary King; Irene Yeh
BUSINESS ANALYST, CONTENT TOOLS Amanda Harmatys
CONTENT OPERATIONS ASSISTANT Shannon Stroud
EDITORIAL SERVICES ADMINISTRATOR Marie Brannon

TEST KITCHEN & FOOD STYLING MANAGER
Sarah Thompson
TEST COOKS Nicholas Iverson (lead), Matthew Hass,
Lauren Knoelke
FOOD STYLISTS Kathryn Conrad (lead), Shannon Roum,
Leah Rekau
PREP COOKS Bethany Van Jacobson (lead), Megumi Garcia,
Melissa Hansen
CULINARY TEAM ASSISTANT Megan Behr

PHOTOGRAPHY DIRECTOR Stephanie Marchese
PHOTOGRAPHERS Dan Roberts, Jim Wieland
PHOTOGRAPHER/SET STYLIST Grace Natoli Sheldon
SET STYLISTS Melissa Franco, Stacey Genaw, Dee Dee Jacq

EDITORIAL BUSINESS MANAGER Kristy Martin
EDITORIAL BUSINESS ASSOCIATE Samantha Lea Stoeger
CONTRIBUTING EDITORIAL BUSINESS ASSISTANT
Andrea Polzin

EDITOR, *TASTE OF HOME* Jeanne Ambrose
ASSOCIATE CREATIVE DIRECTOR, *TASTE OF HOME*
Erin Timmons
ART DIRECTOR, *TASTE OF HOME* Kristin Bowker

BUSINESS
VICE PRESIDENT, GROUP PUBLISHER Kirsten Marchioli
PUBLISHER, *TASTE OF HOME* Donna Lindskog
GENERAL MANAGER, TASTE OF HOME COOKING SCHOOL
Erin Puariea

TRUSTED MEDIA BRANDS, INC.
PRESIDENT AND CHIEF EXECUTIVE OFFICER Bonnie Kintzer
CHIEF FINANCIAL OFFICER/CHIEF OPERATING OFFICER
Howard Halligan
CHIEF REVENUE OFFICER Richard Sutton
CHIEF MARKETING OFFICER Alec Casey
CHIEF DIGITAL OFFICER Vince Errico
CHIEF TECHNOLOGY OFFICER Aneel Tejwaney
SENIOR VICE PRESIDENT, GLOBAL HR & COMMUNICATIONS
Phyllis E. Gebhardt, SPHR; SHRM-SCP
VICE PRESIDENT, DIGITAL CONTENT & AUDIENCE
DEVELOPMENT Diane Dragan
VICE PRESIDENT, MAGAZINE MARKETING Chris Gaydos
VICE PRESIDENT, BUSINESS DEVELOPMENT Beth Gorry
VICE PRESIDENT, FINANCIAL PLANNING & ANALYSIS
William Houston
PUBLISHING DIRECTOR, BOOKS Debra Polansky
VICE PRESIDENT, CONSUMER MARKETING PLANNING
Jim Woods

COVER PHOTOGRAPHY
PHOTOGRAPHER Grace Natoli Sheldon
FOOD STYLIST Leah Rekau
SET STYLIST Stacey Genaw

PICTURED ON THE FRONT COVER: Ravioli Skillet (p. 14)

PICTURED ON THE BACK COVER: Summer Breakfast
Skillet (p. 91); Caramel-Apple Skillet Buckle (p. 95);
Zucchini & Sausage Stovetop Casserole (p. 36)

LIKE US
facebook.com/
tasteofhome

TWEET US
@tasteofhome

FOLLOW US
pinterest.com/taste_
of_home

SHOP WITH US
shoptasteofhome.com

SHARE A RECIPE
tasteofhome.com/submit

THAI CHICKEN
PEANUT NOODLES,
PAGE 28

Make It Sizzle!

It's time to fire up the stovetop! *Taste of Home Skillet Sensations* is here to transform your time in the kitchen. Whether you're making breakfast, lunch, dinner or dessert (yes, really!), turn to your trusty skillet whenever mealtime rolls around.

Inside this book you'll find **181 dishes** sure to satisfy your gang. These tasty recipes come from home cooks like you, so you know they're simple, quick and family-friendly.

If you need a table-ready meal in a half hour, turn to the deliciously easy cover recipe: **Ravioli Skillet (p. 14).** For other 30-minute winners, cook up **Skillet Pork Chops with Apples & Onion (p. 43)** and **Basil-Lemon Crab Linguine (p. 57).**

Guess what? You can keep the skillet out when it's time for dessert! Whip up something sweet and wow loved ones.

Present the stunning **Cornmeal Towers with Strawberries & Cream (p. 98),** or go the cake route and bake **Banana Skillet Upside-Down Cake (p. 97).**

Look for our special icons highlighting recipes throughout this book: FREEZE IT , FAST FIX and 5 INGREDIENTS . Let these recipes guide you to easy solutions for everyday needs.

Also, don't miss the special bonus chapter, full of recipes cooked in a cast-iron skillet over an open flame. These recipes, including **Walking Tacos (p. 107),** will get you through any meal in the great outdoors. Grab your cast iron, pack the cooler and go!

Serving hot and hearty meals has never been easier or faster. No matter what you're looking to cook up, *Skillet Sensations* is here to help!

8

84

50

39

MAKE IT SIZZLE

Look for this icon throughout the book—it'll point out helpful tips and tricks to make the most delicious meals yet, plus some reviews from *Taste of Home* online community members!

**BANANA SKILLET
UPSIDE-DOWN CAKE
PAGE 97**

CONTENTS

LOOK FOR THESE
HANDY ICONS:

FREEZE IT
With a little planning,
you can make these
casserole dishes ahead
of time and simply store
them in your freezer.

5 INGREDIENTS
With the exception of
water, salt, pepper and oil,
these dishes call for only a
few items, many of which
you likely have on hand.

FAST FIX
Eat great even on your
busiest days. Discover
easy recipes that are
table-ready in 30 minutes
or less!

BEEF & SPINACH LO MEIN,
PAGE 11

10

18

17

BEEF &
GROUND BEEF

Come and get it! **Dinner's served** when you plate up one of these sizzling entrees. Find recipes to highlight steaks, ground beef and meatballs in a **delicious new way.**

GREEK BEEF PITAS

FAST FIX

GREEK BEEF PITAS

A local fast-food pita restaurant provided the inspiration for me to make my own Greek-style sandwiches at home. Throw olives on top if you like.

—**NANCY SOUSLEY** LAFAYETTE, IN

START TO FINISH: 25 MIN.
MAKES: 4 SERVINGS

- 1 pound lean ground beef (90% lean)
- 1 small onion, chopped
- 3 garlic cloves, minced
- 1 teaspoon dried oregano
- ¾ teaspoon salt, divided
- 1 cup reduced-fat plain Greek yogurt
- 1 medium tomato, chopped
- ½ cup chopped peeled cucumber
- 1 teaspoon dill weed
- 4 whole pita breads, warmed
   Additional chopped tomatoes and cucumber, optional

1. In a large skillet, cook the beef, onion and garlic over medium heat 8-10 minutes or until the beef is no longer pink and vegetables are tender, breaking up beef into crumbles; drain. Stir in oregano and ½ teaspoon salt.

2. In a small bowl, mix the yogurt, tomato, cucumber, dill and the remaining salt. Spoon ¾ cup beef mixture over each pita bread; top with 3 tablespoons yogurt sauce. If desired, top with additional tomatoes and cucumbers. Serve with remaining yogurt sauce.

SPICY LASAGNA SKILLET DINNER

Skillet lasagna bails me out when I need dinner in a flash. A leafy salad and buttery garlic toast round out the meal.

—DONNA BOOTH TOMAHAWK, KY

START TO FINISH: 30 MIN.
MAKES: 6 SERVINGS

- 1 package (6.4 ounces) lasagna dinner mix
- 1 pound lean ground beef (90% lean)
- 1 large onion, chopped
- 1 medium green pepper, chopped
- 1 garlic clove, minced
- 1 jar (14 ounces) meatless spaghetti sauce
- ½ cup chunky salsa
- 1 teaspoon garlic powder
- 1 teaspoon Italian seasoning
- ½ teaspoon dried thyme
- ½ teaspoon ground cumin
- ¼ teaspoon salt
- ¼ teaspoon crushed red pepper flakes
- 1 cup (4 ounces) shredded mozzarella and provolone cheese blend

1. Fill a large saucepan three-fourths full with water; bring to a boil. Add pasta from lasagna dinner; cook, uncovered, 10-12 minutes or until pasta is tender.

2. Meanwhile, in a large skillet, cook beef, onion, green pepper and garlic over medium heat 6-8 minutes or until beef is no longer pink and vegetables are tender, breaking up beef into crumbles; drain.

3. Stir in the spaghetti sauce, salsa, seasonings and contents of seasoning packet from lasagna dinner. Bring to a boil. Reduce heat; simmer, uncovered, 5 minutes. Remove from heat.

4. Drain pasta. Add to the tomato mixture; toss to coat. Sprinkle with cheese; let stand, covered, until the cheese is melted.

FREEZE OPTION *Freeze cooled pasta mixture and cheese in separate freezer containers. To use, partially thaw in refrigerator overnight. Heat through in a skillet, stirring occasionally and adding a little water if necessary. Remove from heat. Sprinkle with cheese; let stand, covered, until cheese is melted.*

BASIL-BUTTER STEAKS WITH ROASTED POTATOES

BASIL-BUTTER STEAKS WITH ROASTED POTATOES

A few ingredients and 30 minutes are all you'll need for this incredibly satisfying meal. A simply lovely basil butter gives these steaks a very special taste.

—TASTE OF HOME TEST KITCHEN

START TO FINISH: 30 MIN.
MAKES: 4 SERVINGS

- 1 package (15 ounces) frozen Parmesan and roasted garlic red potato wedges
- 4 beef tenderloin steaks (1¼ inches thick and 6 ounces each)
- ½ teaspoon salt
- ½ teaspoon pepper
- 5 tablespoons butter, divided
- 2 cups grape tomatoes
- 1 tablespoon minced fresh basil

1. Bake potato wedges according to package directions.

2. Meanwhile, sprinkle the steaks with salt and pepper. In a 10-inch cast-iron skillet, brown steaks in 2 tablespoons butter. Add tomatoes to skillet. Bake, uncovered, at 425° for 15-20 minutes or until meat reaches desired doneness (for medium-rare, a thermometer should read 145°; medium, 160°; well-done, 170°).

3. In a small bowl, combine basil and remaining butter. Spoon over steaks and serve with potatoes.

SPICY LASAGNA SKILLET DINNER

BRIEF BURRITOS

CASHEW CURRIED BEEF

This recipe is a favorite with my loved ones. The ingredients are a wonderful mix of sweet, salty and spicy.

—**JENNIFER FRIDGEN** EAST GRAND FORKS, MN

PREP: 20 MIN. • **COOK:** 20 MIN.
MAKES: 5 SERVINGS

- 1 **pound beef top sirloin steak, thinly sliced**
- 2 **tablespoons canola oil, divided**
- 1 **can (13.66 ounces) coconut milk, divided**
- 1 **tablespoon red curry paste**
- 2 **tablespoons packed brown sugar**
- 2 **tablespoons fish sauce or soy sauce**
- 8 **cups chopped bok choy**
- 1 **small sweet red pepper, sliced**
- ½ **cup salted cashews**
- ½ **cup minced fresh cilantro**
  Hot cooked brown rice

1. In a large skillet, saute beef in 1 tablespoon oil until no longer pink. Remove from skillet and set aside.
2. Spoon ½ cup cream from top of coconut milk and place in the pan. Add remaining oil; bring to a boil. Add the curry paste; cook and stir for 5 minutes or until oil separates from coconut milk mixture.
3. Stir in the brown sugar, fish sauce and remaining coconut milk. Bring to a boil. Reduce heat; simmer, uncovered, for 5 minutes or until slightly thickened. Add bok choy and red pepper; return to a boil. Cook and stir 2-3 minutes longer or until vegetables are tender.
4. Stir in the cashews, cilantro and beef; heat through. Serve with rice.
NOTE *This recipe was tested with regular (full-fat) coconut milk. Light coconut milk contains less cream.*

FAST FIX

BRIEF BURRITOS

As a busy mom, my evenings are often hectic. I can put these quick burritos together after school. Best of all, my kids love them.

—**GINGER BUROW** FREDERICKSBURG, TX

START TO FINISH: 20 MIN.
MAKES: 8 SERVINGS

- 1 **pound ground beef**
- 1 **can (16 ounces) refried beans**
- 1 **can (10 ounces) diced tomatoes and green chilies, drained**
- ½ **cup chili sauce**
- 8 **flour tortillas (10 inches), warmed**
- ½ **cup shredded cheddar cheese**
- ½ **cup sour cream**

1. In a large skillet, cook beef over medium heat 6-8 minutes or until no longer pink, breaking into crumbles; drain. Stir in beans, tomatoes and chili sauce; heat through.
2. Place about ½ cup meat mixture near the center on each tortilla; top with cheese and sour cream. Fold bottom and sides of tortilla over the filling and roll up. Serve immediately.

---

(5) INGREDIENTS FAST FIX

GARLICKY BEEF & TOMATOES WITH PASTA

A fast pasta and beef dish with spinach and white beans will make your hungry family a happy one.

—**LISA DIFFELL** CORINTH, ME

START TO FINISH: 20 MIN.
MAKES: 6 SERVINGS

- 1 **package (16 ounces) uncooked bow tie pasta**
- 1 **pound ground beef**
- ¼ **teaspoon salt**
- 2 **cans (14½ ounces each) diced tomatoes with roasted garlic, undrained**
- 1 **can (15 ounces) white kidney or cannellini beans, rinsed and drained**
- 1 **package (10 ounces) frozen chopped spinach, thawed and squeezed dry**

Cook pasta according to package directions. Meanwhile, in a large skillet, cook the beef over medium heat 6-8 minutes or until no longer pink, breaking into crumbles; drain. Sprinkle beef with salt. Stir in the remaining ingredients; heat through. Serve with pasta.

BEEF & SPINACH LO MEIN

If you like a good stir-fry, lo mein will definitely satisfy. I discovered this winner at an international luncheon.
—**DENISE PATTERSON** BAINBRIDGE, OH

START TO FINISH: 30 MIN.
MAKES: 5 SERVINGS

- ¼ cup hoisin sauce
- 2 tablespoons soy sauce
- 1 tablespoon water
- 2 teaspoons sesame oil
- 2 garlic cloves, minced
- ¼ teaspoon crushed red pepper flakes
- 1 pound beef top round steak, thinly sliced
- 6 ounces uncooked spaghetti
- 4 teaspoons canola oil, divided
- 1 can (8 ounces) sliced water chestnuts, drained
- 2 green onions, sliced
- 1 package (10 ounces) fresh spinach, coarsely chopped
- 1 red chili pepper, seeded and thinly sliced

1. In a small bowl, mix the first six ingredients. Remove ¼ cup mixture to a large bowl; add beef and toss to coat. Marinate at room temperature 10 minutes.

2. Cook spaghetti according to package directions. Meanwhile, in a large skillet, heat 1½ teaspoons canola oil. Add half of beef mixture; stir-fry 1-2 minutes or until no longer pink. Remove from pan. Repeat with an additional 1½ teaspoons oil and remaining beef mixture.

3. Stir-fry the water chestnuts and green onions in remaining canola oil 30 seconds. Stir in the spinach and remaining hoisin mixture; cook until spinach is wilted. Return beef to pan; heat through.

4. Drain spaghetti; add to the beef mixture and toss to combine. Sprinkle with chili pepper.

NOTE *Wear disposable gloves when cutting hot peppers; the oils can burn skin. Avoid touching your face.*

BEEF & SPINACH
LO MEIN

FAJITA
BURGER
WRAPS

FAJITA BURGER WRAPS

A tender burger, crisp veggies and a crunchy shell, plus lots of fajita flavor—your kids will love it.

—**ANTONIO SMITH** CANAL WINCHESTER, OH

START TO FINISH: 30 MIN.
MAKES: 4 SERVINGS

- 1 **pound lean ground beef (90% lean)**
- 2 **tablespoons fajita seasoning mix**
- 2 **teaspoons canola oil**
- 1 **medium green pepper, cut into thin strips**
- 1 **medium red sweet pepper, cut into thin strips**
- 1 **medium onion, halved and sliced**
- 4 **flour tortillas (10 inches)**
- ¾ **cup shredded cheddar cheese**

1. In a large bowl, combine beef and seasoning mix, mixing lightly but thoroughly. Shape into four ½-in.-thick patties.

2. In a large skillet, heat oil over medium heat. Add the burgers; cook 4 minutes on each side. Remove from pan. In the same skillet, add peppers and onion; cook and stir 5-7 minutes or until lightly browned and tender.

3. On the center of each tortilla, place ½ cup pepper mixture, one burger and 3 tablespoons cheese. Fold sides of tortilla over burger; fold top and bottom to close, forming a square.

4. Wipe skillet clean. Place wraps in skillet, seam side down. Cook on medium heat 1-2 minutes on each side or until golden brown and a thermometer inserted in the beef reads 160°.

KOREAN BEEF
AND RICE

KOREAN BEEF AND RICE

A friend raved about beef cooked in soy sauce and ginger, so I gave it a try. It's absolutely delectable!

—**BETSY KING** DULUTH, MN

START TO FINISH: 15 MIN.
MAKES: 4 SERVINGS

- 1 **pound lean ground beef (90% lean)**
- 3 **garlic cloves, minced**
- ¼ **cup packed brown sugar**
- ¼ **cup reduced-sodium soy sauce**
- 2 **teaspoons sesame oil**
- ¼ **teaspoon ground ginger**
- ¼ **teaspoon crushed red pepper flakes**
- ¼ **teaspoon pepper**
- 2⅔ **cups hot cooked brown rice**
- 3 **green onions, thinly sliced**

1. In a large skillet, cook beef and garlic over medium heat 6-8 minutes or until beef is no longer pink, breaking up beef into crumbles. Meanwhile, in a small bowl, mix the brown sugar, soy sauce, oil and seasonings.
2. Stir sauce into the beef; heat through. Serve with rice. Sprinkle with green onions.
FREEZE OPTION *Freeze cooled meat mixture in freezer containers. To use, partially thaw in refrigerator overnight. Heat through in a saucepan, stirring occasionally.*

MAKE IT SIZZLE

Winner, winner!!! I will definitely put this recipe in my keeper file. I added a little more red pepper flakes and used more scallions.

—**ANNRMS** TASTEOFHOME.COM

PIZZA IN A BOWL

PIZZA IN A BOWL

After spending the day apart, it's a comfort to know that my family can sit down to dinner minutes after we walk in the door. Double this recipe to bring the wow factor to a potluck.

—**VIRGINIA KRITES** CRIDERSVILLE, OH

START TO FINISH: 25 MIN.
MAKES: 6 SERVINGS

- 8 **ounces uncooked rigatoni (about 3 cups)**
- ¾ **pound ground beef**
- ½ **cup chopped onion**
- 1 **can (15 ounces) pizza sauce**
- ⅔ **cup condensed cream of mushroom soup, undiluted**
- 2 **cups (8 ounces) shredded part-skim mozzarella cheese**
- 1 **package (3½ ounces) sliced pepperoni**

1. Cook rigatoni according to package directions; drain. Meanwhile, in a large skillet, cook beef and onion over medium heat 6-8 minutes or until beef is no longer pink, breaking up beef into crumbles; drain. Add pizza sauce, soup and cheese; cook and stir over low heat until cheese is melted.

2. Add rigatoni and pepperoni to the beef mixture. Heat through, stirring to combine.

BEEF TIP STEW OVER FUSILLI

A hearty entree with a well-seasoned veggie blend gets delightful color and flair from fire-roasted tomatoes.

—**TASTE OF HOME** TEST KITCHEN

START TO FINISH: 25 MIN.
MAKES: 4 SERVINGS

- 2½ **cups uncooked fusilli pasta**
- 1 **package (17 ounces) refrigerated beef tips with gravy**
- 1 **package (12 ounces) frozen garlic baby peas and mushrooms blend**
- 1 **can (14½ ounces) fire-roasted diced tomatoes, undrained**
- ½ **teaspoon dried thyme**
- ¼ **teaspoon pepper**

Cook pasta according to package directions. Meanwhile, in a large skillet, combine the beef tips with gravy, vegetable blend, tomatoes, thyme and pepper; heat through. Drain pasta. Serve with beef mixture.

EASY MEATBALL STROGANOFF

RAVIOLI SKILLET

 FAST FIX ▶

EASY MEATBALL STROGANOFF

This recipe has fed not only my own family, but many neighborhood kids! They come running when I make this supper. It's one of those meals you can throw together in a pinch because you know it always works.

—JULIE MAY HATTIESBURG, MS

START TO FINISH: 30 MIN.
MAKES: 4 SERVINGS

- 3 **cups uncooked egg noodles**
- 1 **tablespoon olive oil**
- 1 **package (12 ounces) frozen fully cooked Italian meatballs, thawed**
- 1½ **cups beef broth**
- 1 **teaspoon dried parsley flakes**
- ¾ **teaspoon dried basil**
- ½ **teaspoon salt**
- ½ **teaspoon dried oregano**
- ¼ **teaspoon pepper**
- 1 **cup heavy whipping cream**
- ¾ **cup sour cream**

1. Cook egg noodles according to package directions for al dente; drain.
2. Meanwhile, in a large skillet, heat oil over medium-high heat. Brown meatballs; remove from pan. Add broth, stirring to loosen browned bits from pan. Add seasonings. Bring to a boil; cook 5-7 minutes or until liquid is reduced to ½ cup.
3. Add meatballs, noodles and cream. Bring to a boil. Reduce heat; simmer, covered, 3-5 minutes or until slightly thickened. Stir in sour cream; heat mixture through.

FAST FIX ▶

RAVIOLI SKILLET

Dress up store-bought ravioli and make it really special—prosciutto and mozzarella help to do the trick.

—*TASTE OF HOME* TEST KITCHEN

START TO FINISH: 30 MIN.
MAKES: 4 SERVINGS

- 1 **pound ground beef**
- ¾ **cup chopped green pepper**
- 1 **ounce prosciutto or deli ham, chopped**
- 3 **cups spaghetti sauce**
- ¾ **cup water**
- 1 **package (25 ounces) frozen cheese ravioli**
- 1 **cup (4 ounces) shredded part-skim mozzarella cheese**

1. In a large skillet, cook the beef, green pepper and prosciutto over medium heat until the beef is no longer pink; drain.
2. Stir in the spaghetti sauce and water; bring to a boil. Add ravioli. Reduce heat; cover and simmer for 7-9 minutes or until ravioli is tender, stirring once. Sprinkle with cheese. Simmer, uncovered, 1-2 minutes longer or until cheese is melted.

TENDERLOIN STEAK DIANE

5 INGREDIENTS FAST FIX
MOM'S SLOPPY TACOS

Even on the most hectic weeknight, there's time to serve your family a hearty meal when you can turn to recipes like this one!

—**KAMI JONES** AVONDALE, AZ

START TO FINISH: 30 MIN.
MAKES: 6 SERVINGS

- 1½ **pounds extra-lean ground beef (95% lean)**
- 1 **can (15 ounces) tomato sauce**
- ¾ **teaspoon garlic powder**
- ½ **teaspoon salt**
- ¼ **teaspoon pepper**
- ¼ **teaspoon cayenne pepper**
- 12 **taco shells, warmed**
  Optional toppings: shredded lettuce and cheese, chopped tomatoes, avocado and olives

1. In a large skillet, cook beef over medium heat until no longer pink. Stir in the tomato sauce, garlic powder, salt, pepper and cayenne. Bring to a boil. Reduce heat; simmer, uncovered, for 10 minutes.

2. Fill each taco shell with ¼ cup beef mixture and toppings of your choice.

5 INGREDIENTS FAST FIX
BEEF TIPS WITH HORSERADISH GRAVY

No one will guess that you only spent 25 minutes making dinner. The combo of creme fraiche and horseradish gives the beef tips an exceptional flavor. It's definitely special enough for company.

—**LAURA MAJCHRZAK** HUNT VALLEY, MD

START TO FINISH: 25 MIN.
MAKES: 4 SERVINGS

- 1 **package (17 ounces) refrigerated beef tips with gravy**
- 1 **cup (8 ounces) creme fraiche or sour cream**
- 2 **tablespoons prepared horseradish**
- ¼ **teaspoon pepper**
- 2 **tablespoons minced chives Hot cooked rice**

In a large nonstick skillet, combine the beef tips with gravy, creme fraiche, horseradish and pepper. Cook and stir over medium-low heat until heated through. Sprinkle with chives and serve with rice.

FAST FIX
TENDERLOIN STEAK DIANE

When my son's eating dinner, I make sure to add more mushrooms to this recipe. He loves them, and they are just fantastic with the steak.

—**CAROLYN TURNER** RENO, NV

START TO FINISH: 30 MIN.
MAKES: 4 SERVINGS

- 4 **beef tenderloin steaks (6 ounces each)**
- 1 **teaspoon steak seasoning**
- 2 **tablespoons butter**
- 1 **cup sliced fresh mushrooms**
- ½ **cup reduced-sodium beef broth**
- ¼ **cup heavy whipping cream**
- 1 **tablespoon steak sauce**
- 1 **teaspoon garlic salt with parsley**
- 1 **teaspoon minced chives**

1. Sprinkle the steaks with steak seasoning. In a large skillet, heat butter over medium heat. Add steaks; cook 4-5 minutes on each side or until meat reaches desired doneness (for medium-rare, a thermometer should read 145°; medium, 160°; well-done, 170°). Remove steaks from pan.

2. Add mushrooms to skillet; cook and stir over medium-high heat until tender. Add broth, stirring to loosen browned bits from pan. Stir in cream, steak sauce and garlic salt. Bring to a boil; cook and stir 1-2 minutes or until sauce is slightly thickened.

3. Return steaks to pan; turn to coat and heat through. Stir in chives.

NOTE *This recipe was tested with McCormick's Montreal Steak Seasoning. Look for it in the spice aisle.*

MOM'S SLOPPY TACOS

BEEFY
TORTELLINI
SKILLET

⑤ INGREDIENTS **FAST FIX**

BEEFY TORTELLINI SKILLET

This tortellini skillet wonder is a dish the family craves. From browning the beef to cooking the pasta and melting the cheese, everything happens in one pan.

—**JULI MEYERS** HINESVILLE, GA

START TO FINISH: 20 MIN.
MAKES: 4 SERVINGS

- 1 **pound ground beef**
- ½ **teaspoon Montreal steak seasoning**
- 1 **cup water**
- 1 **teaspoon beef bouillon granules**
- 1 **package (19 ounces) frozen cheese tortellini**
- 1 **cup (4 ounces) shredded Italian cheese blend**

1. In a large skillet, cook beef over medium heat 5-6 minutes or until no longer pink, breaking into crumbles; drain. Stir in steak seasoning. Add the water and bouillon; bring to a boil. Stir in tortellini; return to a boil. Reduce heat; simmer, covered, 3-4 minutes or until tortellini are tender.

2. Remove from heat; sprinkle with cheese. Let stand, covered, until cheese is melted.

SIZZLE & SMOKE FLAT IRON STEAKS

Smoked paprika and chipotle pepper add a Southwestern touch to blackened steak. If you want to cool things off a bit, add a salad of leafy greens with fruit and cheese on the side.

—**DENISE POUNDS** HUTCHINSON, KS

START TO FINISH: 20 MIN.
MAKES: 4 SERVINGS

- 1½ teaspoons smoked paprika
- 1 teaspoon salt
- 1 teaspoon ground chipotle pepper
- ½ teaspoon pepper
- 1¼ pounds beef flat iron steaks or top sirloin steak (¾ inch thick)
- 2 tablespoons butter
  Lime wedges, optional

1. Combine seasonings; rub over steaks. In a large skillet, cook beef in butter over medium-high heat for 30 seconds on each side. Reduce the heat to medium; cook the steaks for 5-7 minutes on each side or until the meat reaches desired doneness (for medium-rare, a thermometer should read 145°; medium, 160°; well-done, 170°).
2. Cut into slices; serve with lime wedges if desired.

PORCUPINE MEATBALLS

I used to clamor for these well-seasoned meatballs in a rich tomato sauce, one of my mom's best recipes. Later I made it for our children, and now my daughters make it for their families.

—**DARLIS WILFER** WEST BEND, WI

PREP: 20 MIN. • **COOK:** 1 HOUR
MAKES: 4-6 SERVINGS

- ½ cup uncooked long grain rice
- ½ cup water
- ⅓ cup chopped onion
- 1 teaspoon salt
- ½ teaspoon celery salt
- ⅛ teaspoon pepper

- ⅛ teaspoon garlic powder
- 1 pound ground beef
- 2 tablespoons canola oil
- 1 can (15 ounces) tomato sauce
- 1 cup water
- 2 tablespoons brown sugar
- 2 teaspoons Worcestershire sauce

In a bowl, combine the first seven ingredients. Add beef and mix well; shape into 1½-in. balls. In a large skillet, brown meatballs in oil; drain. Combine tomato sauce, water, brown sugar and Worcestershire sauce; pour over meatballs. Reduce heat; cover and simmer for 1 hour.

MERLOT FILET MIGNON

Although it is such a simple recipe, you can feel confident serving this filet to your guests. The rich sauce adds a touch of elegance. Just add a salad and rolls.

—**JAUNEEN HOSKING** WATERFORD, WI

START TO FINISH: 20 MIN.
MAKES: 2 SERVINGS

- 2 beef tenderloin steaks (8 ounces each)
- 3 tablespoons butter, divided
- 1 tablespoon olive oil
- 1 cup merlot
- 2 tablespoons heavy whipping cream
- ⅛ teaspoon salt

1. In a small skillet, cook the steaks in 1 tablespoon butter and oil over medium heat for 4-6 minutes on each side or until the meat reaches desired doneness (for medium-rare, a thermometer should read 145°; medium, 160°; well-done, 170°). Remove and keep warm.
2. In the same skillet, add the wine, stirring to loosen browned bits from pan. Bring to a boil; cook until liquid is reduced to ¼ cup. Add the cream, salt and remaining butter; bring to a boil. Cook and stir for 1-2 minutes or until slightly thickened and the butter is melted. Serve with steaks.

CHILI HASH

CHILI HASH

You'll need to use your microwave and stovetop for only a few minutes to make a comforting meal on a busy night.

—*TASTE OF HOME* TEST KITCHEN

START TO FINISH: 30 MIN.
MAKES: 4 SERVINGS

- 1 pound medium potatoes, cubed
- ½ cup water
- 1 pound ground beef
- 1 medium onion, chopped
- 1 can (15½ ounces) chili starter
- 1 cup frozen peas
- 2 tablespoons minced fresh parsley
- ¼ teaspoon salt
  Sour cream, optional

1. Place potatoes and water in a microwave-safe dish. Cover and microwave on high for 7 minutes or until tender.
2. Meanwhile, in a large skillet, cook beef and onion over medium heat until meat is no longer pink; drain. Drain potatoes and add to the skillet. Stir in the chili starter, peas, parsley and salt. Bring to a boil. Reduced heat; simmer, uncovered, for 5 minutes. Serve with sour cream if desired.

**SKILLET BBQ
BEEF POTPIE**

PEPPER STEAK
WITH POTATOES

I added potatoes to a favorite Asian pepper steak recipe. Now this meaty skillet dish satisfies everyone in my house full of hungry guys.

—**KRISTINE MARRA** CLIFTON PARK, NY

START TO FINISH: 30 MIN.
MAKES: 6 SERVINGS

- 1½ **pounds red potatoes (about 5 medium), sliced**
- ½ **cup water**
- 1 **cup beef broth**
- 4 **teaspoons cornstarch**
- ⅛ **teaspoon pepper**
- 2 **tablespoons olive oil, divided**
- 1 **pound beef top sirloin steak, thinly sliced**
- 1 **garlic clove, minced**
- 1 **medium green pepper, julienned**
- 1 **small onion, chopped**

1. Place potatoes and water in a large microwave-safe dish. Microwave, covered, on high for 5-7 minutes or until tender.

2. Meanwhile, in a small bowl, mix broth, cornstarch and pepper until smooth. In a large skillet, heat 1 tablespoon oil over medium-high heat. Add the beef; cook and stir 2-3 minutes or until no longer pink. Add garlic; cook 1 minute longer. Remove from pan.

3. In same pan, heat remaining oil. Add green pepper and onion; cook and stir until vegetables are crisp-tender. Stir cornstarch mixture and add to pan. Bring to a boil; cook and stir 1-2 minutes or until sauce is thickened. Add potatoes and beef to pan; heat through.

SKILLET BBQ
BEEF POTPIE

Beef potpie is a classic comfort food, but who's got time to see it through? My crowd-pleaser is not only speedy; it uses up leftover stuffing.

—**PRISCILLA YEE** CONCORD, CA

START TO FINISH: 25 MIN.
MAKES: 4 SERVINGS

- 1 **pound lean ground beef (90% lean)**
- ⅓ **cup thinly sliced green onions, divided**
- 2 **cups frozen mixed vegetables, thawed**
- ½ **cup salsa**
- ½ **cup barbecue sauce**
- 3 **cups cooked corn bread stuffing**
- ½ **cup shredded cheddar cheese**
- ¼ **cup chopped sweet red pepper**

1. In a large skillet, cook beef and ¼ cup green onions over medium heat 6-8 minutes or until beef is no longer pink, breaking into crumbles; drain. Stir in mixed vegetables, salsa and barbecue sauce; cook, covered, over medium-low heat 4-5 minutes or until heated through.

2. Layer stuffing over the beef; sprinkle with cheese, red pepper and remaining green onion. Cook, covered, 3-5 minutes longer or until heated through and cheese is melted.

MAKE IT SIZZLE

When we have extra steak, I make a quick stew. First, I cut it into small cubes and brown in olive oil in a skillet. Then I stir in some flour until blended. Next, I add 2 cubed potatoes, 3 sliced carrots, a large diced onion, 2 cups of water and 2 beef bouillon cubes. I simmer it until the vegetables are done, stirring frequently.

—**JEANETTE S.** ST. GEORGE, KS

CHICKEN-FRIED STEAK & GRAVY

When I was a child, my grandmother taught me Texas-style chicken-fried steak. Of course, I taught my daughters, and when my granddaughters are older, I'll be sure to show them, too.
—**DONNA CATER** FORT ANN, NY

START TO FINISH: 30 MIN.
MAKES: 4 SERVINGS

- 1¼ cups all-purpose flour, divided
- 2 large eggs
- 1½ cups 2% milk, divided
- 4 beef cubed steaks (6 ounces each)
- 1¼ teaspoons salt, divided
- 1 teaspoon pepper, divided
  Oil for frying
- 1 cup water

1. Place 1 cup flour in a shallow bowl. In a separate shallow bowl, whisk the eggs and ½ cup milk until blended. Sprinkle steaks with ¾ teaspoon each salt and pepper. Dip in flour to coat both sides; shake off excess. Dip in egg mixture, then again in flour.

2. In a large skillet, heat ¼ in. of oil over medium heat. Add steaks; cook 4-6 minutes on each side or until golden brown and a thermometer reads 160°. Remove from pan; drain on paper towels. Keep warm.

3. Remove all but 2 tablespoons oil from the pan. Stir in the remaining ¼ cup flour, ½ teaspoon salt and ¼ teaspoon pepper until smooth; cook and stir over medium heat 3-4 minutes or until golden brown. Gradually whisk in water and remaining milk. Bring to a boil, stirring constantly; cook and stir 1-2 minutes or until thickened. Serve with steaks.

DIJON BEEF TENDERLOIN

DIJON BEEF TENDERLOIN

I like having an ace recipe up my sleeve, and tenderloin with Dijon is my go-to for everything from birthdays to buffets to holidays. It's a winner.
—**DONNA LINDECAMP** MORGANTON, NC

START TO FINISH: 20 MIN.
MAKES: 4 SERVINGS

- 4 beef tenderloin steaks (1 inch thick and 4 ounces each)
- ½ teaspoon salt
- ¼ teaspoon pepper
- 5 tablespoons butter, divided
- 1 large onion, halved and thinly sliced
- 1 cup beef stock
- 1 tablespoon Dijon mustard

1. Sprinkle steaks with salt and pepper. In a large skillet, heat 2 tablespoons butter over medium-high heat. Add the steaks; cook 4-6 minutes on each side or until meat reaches desired doneness (for medium-rare, a thermometer should read 145°; medium, 160°; well-done, 170°). Remove from pan; keep warm.

2. In the same pan, heat 1 tablespoon butter over medium heat. Add onion; cook and stir 4-6 minutes or until tender. Stir in stock; bring to a boil. Cook 1-2 minutes or until liquid is reduced by half. Stir in mustard; remove from heat. Cube remaining butter; stir into sauce just until blended. Serve with steaks.

**TURKEY SALISBURY STEAKS,
PAGE 31**

23

33

30

CHICKEN & TURKEY

Bring on the sizzle! Take your next meal from **zero to hero** in just a few minutes. Grab your skillet to fry up some **juicy chicken** and veggies all in one. Or maybe you're in the mood for a **turkey and pasta** combo. Either way, you win!

GRAM'S FRIED CHICKEN

GRAM'S FRIED CHICKEN

Growing up, I always looked forward to enjoying my grandmother's fried chicken. I never knew exactly how she made it, but my crispy recipe using potato flakes is pretty close.

—DAVID NELSON LINCOLNTON, NC

PREP: 20 MIN. + CHILLING • **COOK:** 10 MIN.
MAKES: 4 SERVINGS

- 1 large egg
- 1 cup 2% milk
- 2 cups mashed potato flakes
- 1 tablespoon garlic powder
- 1 tablespoon each dried oregano, parsley flakes and minced onion
- ½ teaspoon salt
- ¼ teaspoon coarsely ground pepper
- 4 boneless skinless chicken breast halves (6 ounces each)
  Oil for frying

1. In a shallow bowl, whisk egg and milk. In another shallow bowl, toss the potato flakes with seasonings. Remove half of mixture and reserve (for a second coat of breading).
2. Pound chicken with a meat mallet to ½-in. thickness. Dip chicken in egg mixture, then in potato mixture, patting to help coating adhere. Arrange chicken in an even layer on a large plate. Cover and refrigerate chicken and remaining egg mixture 1 hour. Discard the remaining used potato mixture.
3. In a 12-in. cast-iron or other deep skillet, heat ½ in. of oil over medium heat to 350°. For the second coat of breading, dip chicken in remaining egg mixture, then in unused potato mixture; pat to coat. Fry the chicken 4-5 minutes on each side or until golden brown and chicken is no longer pink. Drain on paper towels.

DID YOU KNOW?
Cast-iron skillets are great for cooking because they can handle the heat, but they need special care for cleaning. Never submerge a hot cast-iron skillet in cold water, or it may crack. Also, don't use dish soap when washing— it'll remove the seasoning.

TURKEY TORTELLINI TOSS

FAST FIX

TURKEY TORTELLINI TOSS

One night I had no clue what to make for dinner, but I knew I had some frozen tortellini on hand. After quickly scanning the cupboards and refrigerator for more ingredients, soon I was cooking away!

—**LEO PARR** NEW ORLEANS, LA

START TO FINISH: 30 MIN.
MAKES: 4 SERVINGS

- 2 **cups frozen cheese tortellini (about 8 ounces)**
- 1 **pound ground turkey**
- 2 **medium zucchini, halved lengthwise and sliced**
- 2 **garlic cloves, minced**
- 1½ **cups cherry tomatoes, halved**
- 1 **teaspoon dried oregano**
- ½ **teaspoon salt**
- ¼ **teaspoon crushed red pepper flakes**
- 1 **cup shredded Asiago cheese, divided**
- 1 **tablespoon olive oil**

1. Cook the tortellini according to package directions.
2. Meanwhile, in a large skillet, cook the turkey, zucchini and garlic over medium heat 7-9 minutes or until turkey is no longer pink, breaking up turkey into crumbles; drain. Add tomatoes, oregano, salt and pepper flakes; cook 2 minutes longer. Stir in ¾ cup cheese.
3. Drain tortellini; add to skillet and toss to combine. Drizzle with the oil; sprinkle with remaining cheese.

FAST FIX

ITALIAN TURKEY SKILLET

I try to find imaginative ways to use leftovers, especially turkey. This pasta toss is lightly coated with tomato sauce and accented with fresh mushrooms.

—**PATRICIA KILE** ELIZABETHTOWN, PA

START TO FINISH: 20 MIN.
MAKES: 8 SERVINGS

- 1 **package (16 ounces) linguine**
- 2 **tablespoons canola oil**
- ¾ **cup sliced fresh mushrooms**
- 1 **medium onion, chopped**
- 1 **celery rib, chopped**
- 1 **small green pepper, chopped**
- 2 **cups cubed cooked turkey**
- 1 **can (14½ ounces) diced tomatoes, drained**
- 1 **can (10¾ ounces) condensed tomato soup, undiluted**
- 1 **tablespoon Italian seasoning**
- 1 **tablespoon minced fresh parsley**
- ¼ **teaspoon pepper**
- ⅛ **teaspoon salt**
- 1 **cup (4 ounces) shredded cheddar cheese, optional**

1. Cook the linguine according to package directions. Meanwhile, in a large skillet, heat oil over medium-high heat. Add mushrooms, onion, celery and green pepper; cook and stir until tender. Stir in turkey, tomatoes, soup and seasonings; heat through.
2. Drain linguine; add to the turkey mixture and toss to combine. If desired, sprinkle with cheese and let stand, covered, until cheese is melted.

ITALIAN TURKEY SKILLET

CAESAR CHICKEN WITH FETA

FAST FIX ▶

SPEEDY CHICKEN MARSALA

This is one of my favorite dishes to order when dining out at restaurants, and so I created an easy version to make in a flash for weeknight dinners at home.

—TRISHA KRUSE EAGLE, ID

START TO FINISH: 30 MIN.
MAKES: 4 SERVINGS

- 8 ounces uncooked whole wheat or multigrain angel hair pasta
- 4 boneless skinless chicken breast halves (5 ounces each)
- ¼ cup all-purpose flour
- 1 teaspoon lemon-pepper seasoning
- ½ teaspoon salt
- 2 tablespoons olive oil, divided
- 4 cups sliced fresh mushrooms
- 1 garlic clove, minced
- 1 cup dry Marsala wine

1. Cook pasta according to package directions. Pound chicken with a meat mallet to ¼-in. thickness. In a large resealable plastic bag, mix the flour, lemon-pepper and salt. Add chicken, one piece at a time; close bag and shake to coat.
2. In a large skillet, heat 1 tablespoon oil over medium heat. Add chicken; cook for 4-5 minutes on each side or until no longer pink. Remove from the pan.
3. In the same skillet, heat the remaining oil over medium-high heat. Add mushrooms; cook and stir until tender. Add garlic; cook 1 minute longer. Add wine; bring to a boil. Cook for 5-6 minutes or until liquid is reduced by half, stirring to loosen browned bits from pan. Return chicken to pan, turning to coat with sauce; heat through.
4. Drain the pasta; serve with the chicken mixture.

---

⑤ INGREDIENTS FAST FIX ▶

CAESAR CHICKEN WITH FETA

My tomato-topped chicken is the right answer on those crazy days when supper has to be on the table in 30 minutes. And it doesn't hurt that it's delicious, too.

—DENISE CHELPKA PHOENIX, AZ

START TO FINISH: 10 MIN.
MAKES: 4 SERVINGS

- 4 boneless skinless chicken breast halves (4 ounces each)
- ½ teaspoon salt
- ¼ teaspoon pepper
- 2 teaspoons olive oil
- 1 medium tomato, chopped
- ¼ cup creamy Caesar salad dressing
- ½ cup crumbled feta cheese

Sprinkle the chicken with salt and pepper. In a large skillet, heat oil over medium-high heat. Brown chicken on one side. Turn chicken; add tomato and salad dressing to skillet. Cook, covered, for 6-8 minutes or until a thermometer inserted in the chicken reads 165°. Sprinkle with cheese.

GOBBLER CAKES

I watched a chef make crab cakes and decided to try it myself with turkey and stuffing. Now the kids request them year-round!

—SUZEE KREBS BRIELLE, NJ

PREP: 25 MIN. • **COOK:** 10 MIN./BATCH
MAKES: 4 SERVINGS

- 1 large egg
- 2 cups cooked stuffing
- 1¼ cups finely chopped cooked turkey
- ½ cup dried cranberries
- ¼ cup mayonnaise
- ½ cup crushed cornflakes
- 1 tablespoon canola oil
  Cranberry sauce and turkey gravy, optional

1. In a large bowl, mix egg, stuffing, turkey, cranberries and mayonnaise. Shape into eight ½-in.-thick patties. Coat with crushed cornflakes.
2. In a large skillet, heat oil over medium heat. Add patties in batches; cook 3-4 minutes on each side or until golden brown. Serve warm, with cranberry sauce and gravy if desired.

CARIBBEAN CHICKEN STIR-FRY

CHICKEN SAUSAGE & GNOCCHI SKILLET

⑤ INGREDIENTS **FAST FIX**

CARIBBEAN CHICKEN STIR-FRY

Fruit cocktail in stir-fry? You'll be surprised by how good this dish is. It's a promising option when time's tight.

—**JEANNE HOLT** MENDOTA HEIGHTS, MN

START TO FINISH: 25 MIN.
MAKES: 4 SERVINGS

- 2 **teaspoons cornstarch**
- ¼ **cup water**
- 1 **pound boneless skinless chicken breasts, cut into ½-inch strips**
- 2 **teaspoons Caribbean jerk seasoning**
- 1 **can (15 ounces) mixed tropical fruit, drained and coarsely chopped**
- 2 **packages (8.8 ounces each) ready-to-serve brown rice**

1. In a small bowl, mix cornstarch and water until smooth.
2. Coat a large skillet with cooking spray; heat over medium-high heat. Add chicken; sprinkle with jerk seasoning. Stir-fry 3-5 minutes or until no longer pink. Stir cornstarch mixture and add to pan with fruit. Bring to a boil; cook and stir 1-2 minutes or until sauce is thickened.
3. Meanwhile, heat rice according to package directions. Serve with the chicken.

FAST FIX

CHICKEN SAUSAGE & GNOCCHI SKILLET

I had a bunch of fresh veggies and combined them with sausage, gnocchi and goat cheese when I needed a quick dinner. Mix and match the ingredients you want for unique results to fit your family.

—**DAHLIA ABRAMS** DETROIT, MI

START TO FINISH: 30 MIN.
MAKES: 4 SERVINGS

- 1 **package (16 ounces) potato gnocchi**
- 1 **tablespoon butter**
- 1 **tablespoon olive oil**
- 2 **fully cooked Italian chicken sausage links (3 ounces each), sliced**
- ½ **pound sliced baby portobello mushrooms**
- 1 **medium onion, finely chopped**
- 1 **pound fresh asparagus, trimmed and cut into ½-inch pieces**
- 2 **garlic cloves, minced**
- 2 **tablespoons white wine or chicken broth**
- 2 **ounces herbed fresh goat cheese**
- 2 **tablespoons minced fresh basil or 2 teaspoons dried basil**
- 1 **tablespoon lemon juice**
- ¼ **teaspoon salt**
- ⅛ **teaspoon pepper**
  Grated Parmesan cheese

1. Cook gnocchi according to the package directions; drain. Meanwhile, in a large skillet, heat butter and oil over medium-high heat. Add sausage, mushrooms and onion; cook and stir until the sausage is browned and the vegetables are tender. Add asparagus and garlic; cook and stir 2-3 minutes longer.
2. Stir in wine. Bring to a boil; cook until liquid is almost evaporated. Add goat cheese, basil, lemon juice, salt and pepper. Stir in the gnocchi; heat through. Sprinkle with the Parmesan cheese.

CHEESY CHICKEN & BROCCOLI ORZO

FLAVORFUL CHICKEN FAJITAS

Fajita nights will become a new tradition once you've served this dish. After letting the chicken marinate for a bit, you're just a few minutes away from this sizzling, savory dinner!

—**JULIE STERCHI** CAMPBELLSVILLE, KY

PREP: 20 MIN. + MARINATING • **COOK:** 5 MIN.
MAKES: 6 SERVINGS

- 4 tablespoons canola oil, divided
- 2 tablespoons lemon juice
- 1½ teaspoons seasoned salt
- 1½ teaspoons dried oregano
- 1½ teaspoons ground cumin
- 1 teaspoon garlic powder
- ½ teaspoon chili powder
- ½ teaspoon paprika
- ½ teaspoon crushed red pepper flakes, optional
- 1½ pounds boneless skinless chicken breast, cut into thin strips
- ½ medium sweet red pepper, julienned
- ½ medium green pepper, julienned
- 4 green onions, thinly sliced
- ½ cup chopped onion
- 6 flour tortillas (8 inches), warmed
   Shredded cheddar cheese, taco sauce, salsa, guacamole and sour cream

1. In a large resealable plastic bag, combine 2 tablespoons oil, lemon juice and seasonings; add the chicken. Seal and turn to coat; refrigerate for 1-4 hours.
2. In a large skillet, saute the peppers and onions in remaining oil until crisp-tender. Remove and keep warm.
3. Discard marinade. In the same skillet, cook chicken over medium-high heat for 5-6 minutes or until no longer pink. Return pepper mixture to pan; heat through.
4. Spoon filling down the center of tortillas; fold in half. Serve with the cheese, taco sauce, salsa, guacamole and sour cream.

CHICKEN VEGGIE SKILLET

I invented this chicken and veggie dish to put extra mushrooms and asparagus to good use. My husband suggested I write the recipe down because it's a keeper.

—**REBEKAH BEYER** SABETHA, KS

START TO FINISH: 30 MIN.
MAKES: 6 SERVINGS

- 1½ pounds boneless skinless chicken breasts, cut into ½-inch strips
- ½ teaspoon salt
- ¼ teaspoon pepper
- 6 teaspoons olive oil, divided
- ½ pound sliced fresh mushrooms
- 1 small onion, halved and sliced
- 2 garlic cloves, minced
- 1 pound fresh asparagus, trimmed and cut into 1-inch pieces
- ½ cup sherry or chicken stock
- 2 tablespoons cold butter, cubed

1. Sprinkle the chicken with salt and pepper. In a large skillet, heat 1 teaspoon oil over medium-high heat. Add half of the chicken; cook and stir 3-4 minutes or until no longer pink. Remove from the pan. Repeat with 1 teaspoon oil and remaining chicken.
2. In same pan, heat 2 teaspoons oil. Add the mushrooms and onion; cook and stir 2-3 minutes or until tender. Add garlic; cook 1 minute longer. Add to the chicken.
3. Heat remaining oil in pan. Add asparagus; cook 2-3 minutes or until crisp-tender. Add the asparagus to chicken and mushrooms.
4. Add sherry to skillet, stirring to loosen browned bits from pan. Bring to a boil; cook 1-2 minutes or until liquid is reduced to 2 tablespoons. Return chicken and vegetables to pan; heat through. Remove from heat; stir in butter, 1 tablespoon at a time.

---

⑤ INGREDIENTS **FAST FIX**

CHEESY CHICKEN & BROCCOLI ORZO

Broccoli and rice casserole tops my family's comfort food list, but when we need something fast, this is it. Cooking chicken and veggie orzo on the stovetop speeds everything up.

—**MARY SHIVERS** ADA, OK

START TO FINISH: 30 MIN.
MAKES: 6 SERVINGS

- 1¼ cups uncooked orzo pasta
- 2 packages (10 ounces each) frozen broccoli with cheese sauce
- 2 tablespoons butter
- 1½ pounds boneless skinless chicken breasts, cut into ½-inch cubes
- 1 medium onion, chopped
- ¾ teaspoon salt
- ½ teaspoon pepper

1. Cook orzo according to package directions. Meanwhile, heat the broccoli with cheese sauce according to package directions.
2. In a large skillet, heat butter over medium heat. Add chicken, onion, salt and pepper; cook and stir 6-8 minutes or until chicken is no longer pink and onion is tender. Drain orzo. Stir the orzo and broccoli with cheese sauce into skillet; heat through.

FAVORITE SKILLET LASAGNA

Whole wheat noodles and zucchini pump up the nutrition in this easy dinner, while ricotta makes it look and taste indulgent.

—LORIE MINER KAMAS, UT

START TO FINISH: 30 MIN.
MAKES: 5 SERVINGS

- ½ pound Italian turkey sausage links, casings removed
- 1 small onion, chopped
- 1 jar (14 ounces) spaghetti sauce
- 2 cups uncooked whole wheat egg noodles
- 1 cup water
- ½ cup chopped zucchini
- ½ cup fat-free ricotta cheese
- 2 tablespoons grated Parmesan cheese
- 1 tablespoon minced fresh parsley or 1 teaspoon dried parsley flakes
- ½ cup shredded part-skim mozzarella cheese

1. In a large nonstick skillet, cook sausage and onion over medium heat until no longer pink, breaking up sausage into crumbles; drain. Stir in spaghetti sauce, noodles, water and zucchini. Bring to a boil. Reduce heat; simmer, covered, 8-10 minutes or until noodles are tender, stirring the mixture occasionally.

2. In a small bowl, combine ricotta cheese, Parmesan cheese and parsley. Drop by tablespoonfuls over pasta mixture. Sprinkle with mozzarella cheese; cook, covered, 3-5 minutes longer or until the cheese is melted.

MAKE IT SIZZLE

Very yummy! I added extra spices—garlic powder, dried basil, oregano, salt and pepper—but it depends on the spaghetti sauce you use. I also added some chopped mushrooms that I needed to use up.

—MOTPC TASTEOFHOME.COM

CHICKEN VEGGIE SKILLET

FAVORITE SKILLET LASAGNA

**THAI CHICKEN
PEANUT NOODLES**

THAI CHICKEN PEANUT NOODLES

My husband loves the spicy Thai flavors in this speedy dish. Break out the chopsticks like he does if you want to have a more immersed dining experience.

—JENNIFER FISHER AUSTIN, TX

START TO FINISH: 30 MIN.
MAKES: 6 SERVINGS

- ¼ **cup creamy peanut butter**
- ½ **cup reduced-sodium chicken broth**
- ¼ **cup lemon juice**
- ¼ **cup reduced-sodium soy sauce**
- 4 **teaspoons Sriracha Asian hot chili sauce**
- ¼ **teaspoon crushed red pepper flakes**
- 12 **ounces uncooked multigrain spaghetti**
- 1 **pound lean ground chicken**
- 1½ **cups julienned carrots**
- 1 **medium sweet red pepper, chopped**
- 1 **garlic clove, minced**
- ½ **cup finely chopped unsalted peanuts**
- 4 **green onions, chopped**

1. In a small bowl, whisk the first six ingredients until blended. Cook spaghetti according to the package directions; drain.

2. Meanwhile, in a large skillet, cook chicken, carrots, pepper and garlic over medium heat 5-6 minutes or until the chicken is no longer pink, breaking up the chicken into crumbles; drain.

3. Stir in the peanut butter mixture; bring to a boil. Reduce heat; simmer, uncovered, 3-5 minutes or until sauce is slightly thickened. Serve with the spaghetti. Top with the peanuts and green onions.

TURKEY MOLE TACOS

In contrast to traditional tacos, these don't need any extra toppings. I've also used bite-sized pieces of chicken thighs instead of ground meat, increasing the cooking time accordingly.

—HELEN GLAZIER SEATTLE, WA

PREP: 25 MIN. • **COOK:** 20 MIN.
MAKES: 6 SERVINGS

- 1¼ pounds lean ground turkey
- 1 celery rib, chopped
- 4 green onions, chopped
- 2 garlic cloves, minced
- 1 can (14½ ounces) diced tomatoes, undrained
- 1 jar (7 ounces) roasted sweet red peppers, drained and chopped
- 2 ounces 53% cacao dark baking chocolate, chopped
- 4 teaspoons chili powder
- 1 teaspoon ground cumin
- ½ teaspoon salt
- ¼ teaspoon ground cinnamon
- ¼ cup lightly salted mixed nuts, coarsely chopped
- 12 corn tortillas (6 inches), warmed

1. In a large nonstick skillet coated with cooking spray, cook the turkey, celery, green onions and garlic over medium heat until meat is no longer pink and vegetables are tender; drain.
2. Stir in the tomatoes, red peppers, chocolate, chili powder, cumin, salt and cinnamon. Bring to a boil. Reduce the heat; cover and simmer for 10 minutes, stirring occasionally.
3. Remove from the heat; stir in the nuts. Place about ⅓ cup of the filling on each tortilla.

FREEZE OPTION *Freeze the cooled meat mixture in freezer containers. To use, partially thaw in refrigerator overnight. Heat through in a saucepan, stirring occasionally and adding a little water if necessary.*

CHEESY ONION CHICKEN SKILLET

My zesty chicken with peppers and onions is so versatile, it works when you serve it over rice, potatoes, noodles or even on a hoagie bun.

—KIM JOHNSON SIBLEY, IA

START TO FINISH: 20 MIN.
MAKES: 4 SERVINGS

- 1 pound boneless skinless chicken breasts, cubed
- 2 teaspoons Mrs. Dash Garlic & Herb seasoning blend
- 2 tablespoons olive oil, divided
- 1 medium green pepper, cut into strips
- ½ medium onion, sliced
- 1 cup (4 ounces) shredded Colby-Monterey Jack cheese

1. Toss the chicken with seasoning blend. In a large nonstick skillet, heat 1 tablespoon oil over medium-high heat. Add the chicken; cook and stir 5-7 minutes or until no longer pink. Remove from pan. In same pan, add remaining oil, pepper and onion; cook and stir 3-4 minutes or until crisp-tender.
2. Stir in the chicken; sprinkle with cheese. Remove from heat; let stand, covered, until cheese is melted.

GORGONZOLA & ORANGE CHICKEN TENDERS

My mom likes to make this for family gatherings, and we all enjoy eating it. Marmalade and Gorgonzola might sound like an unusual combo, but they actually make a great pair.

—YVETTE GORMAN DENVER, PA

START TO FINISH: 25 MIN.
MAKES: 4 SERVINGS

- 1 large egg
- ¼ teaspoon salt
- ¾ cup seasoned bread crumbs
- 1 pound chicken tenderloins
- 2 tablespoons olive oil
- ¼ cup orange marmalade, warmed
- ¼ cup crumbled Gorgonzola cheese

1. In a shallow bowl, whisk egg and salt. Place bread crumbs in another shallow bowl. Dip chicken in the egg, then in bread crumbs, patting to help coating adhere.
2. In a large skillet, heat oil over medium heat. Add chicken; cook 3-4 minutes on each side or until chicken is no longer pink. Drizzle with warm marmalade; top with cheese. Remove from heat; let stand, covered, until cheese begins to melt.

BLUEBERRY-DIJON CHICKEN

Maybe blueberries and chicken together don't seem like a natural fit, but prepare to be dazzled. I add a sprinkling of minced fresh basil as the finishing touch.

—SUSAN MARSHALL COLORADO SPRINGS, CO

START TO FINISH: 30 MIN.
MAKES: 4 SERVINGS

- 4 boneless skinless chicken breast halves (6 ounces each)
- ¼ teaspoon salt
- ¼ teaspoon pepper
- 1 tablespoon butter
- ½ cup blueberry preserves
- ⅓ cup raspberry vinegar
- ¼ cup fresh or frozen blueberries
- 3 tablespoons Dijon mustard
  Minced fresh basil or tarragon, optional

1. Sprinkle chicken with salt and pepper. In a large skillet, cook the chicken in butter over medium heat for 6-8 minutes on each side or until a thermometer reads 170°. Remove and keep warm.
2. In the same skillet, combine the preserves, vinegar, blueberries and mustard, stirring to loosen browned bits from pan. Bring to a boil; cook and stir until thickened. Serve with chicken. Sprinkle with basil if desired.

QUICK CHICKEN & BROCCOLI STIR-FRY

This Asian stir-fry is a suppertime best bet. The spicy sauce works with chicken, seafood, pork or beef. Add whatever veggies you have on hand.

—**KRISTIN RIMKUS** SNOHOMISH, WA

START TO FINISH: 25 MIN.
MAKES: 4 SERVINGS

- 2 **tablespoons rice vinegar**
- 2 **tablespoons mirin (sweet rice wine)**
- 2 **tablespoons chili garlic sauce**
- 1 **tablespoon cornstarch**
- 1 **tablespoon reduced-sodium soy sauce**
- 2 **teaspoons fish sauce or additional soy sauce**
- ½ **cup reduced-sodium chicken broth, divided**
- 2 **cups instant brown rice**
- 2 **teaspoons sesame oil**
- 4 **cups fresh broccoli florets**
- 2 **cups cubed cooked chicken**
- 2 **green onions, sliced**

1. In a small bowl, mix the first six ingredients and ¼ cup chicken broth until smooth. Cook rice according to package directions.
2. Meanwhile, in a large skillet, heat the oil over medium-high heat. Add broccoli; stir-fry 2 minutes. Add the remaining broth; cook 1-2 minutes or until broccoli is crisp-tender. Stir sauce mixture and add to pan. Bring to a boil; cook and stir 1-2 minutes or until sauce is thickened.
3. Stir in chicken and green onions; heat through. Serve with rice.

QUICK CHICKEN & BROCCOLI STIR-FRY

SKILLET CHICKEN WITH OLIVES

SKILLET CHICKEN WITH OLIVES

While I was visiting my cousin in Italy, she made this heavenly chicken for lunch. Now it's a family favorite stateside, too.

—**JOSEPH PISANO** REVERE, MA

START TO FINISH: 20 MIN.
MAKES: 4 SERVINGS

- 4 **boneless skinless chicken thighs (about 1 pound)**
- 1 **teaspoon dried rosemary, crushed**
- ½ **teaspoon pepper**
- ¼ **teaspoon salt**
- 1 **tablespoon olive oil**
- ½ **cup pimiento-stuffed olives, coarsely chopped**
- ¼ **cup white wine or chicken broth**
- 1 **tablespoon drained capers, optional**

1. Sprinkle chicken with rosemary, pepper and salt. In a large skillet, heat oil over medium-high heat. Brown chicken on both sides.
2. Add olives, wine and, if desired, capers. Reduce heat; simmer, covered, 2-3 minutes or until a thermometer inserted in chicken reads 170°.

HONEY MUSTARD APPLE CHICKEN SAUSAGE

I threw this recipe together one day for a fantastic meal. It's a great way to use leftover sausage and rice from dinner the night before.

—**JULIE PUDERBAUGH** BERWICK, PA

START TO FINISH: 20 MIN.
MAKES: 4 SERVINGS

- ¼ **cup honey mustard**
- 2 **tablespoons apple jelly**
- 1 **tablespoon water**
- 1 **tablespoon olive oil**
- 2 **medium apples, sliced**
- 1 **package (12 ounces) fully cooked apple chicken sausage links or flavor of your choice, sliced**
  Hot cooked rice

1. In a small bowl, whisk honey mustard, jelly and water until blended. In a large skillet, heat the oil over medium heat. Add apples; cook and stir 2-3 minutes or until tender. Remove from pan.
2. Add sausage to skillet; cook and stir 2-4 minutes or until browned. Return apples to skillet. Add the mustard mixture; cook and stir 1-2 minutes or until thickened. Serve with rice.

TURKEY SALISBURY STEAKS

My mother always made Salisbury steak. When I married, I developed my own, and it's one my husband requests the most.

—LEANN DOYLE PATCHOGUE, NY

PREP: 20 MIN. • **COOK:** 15 MIN.
MAKES: 4 SERVINGS

- ⅔ cup seasoned bread crumbs, divided
- ⅓ cup finely chopped onion
- 2 teaspoons low-sodium Worcestershire sauce
- 2 teaspoons A.1. steak sauce
- 1 garlic clove, minced
- ½ teaspoon dried basil
- ½ teaspoon dried oregano
- ¼ teaspoon garlic powder
- ¼ teaspoon pepper
- 1 pound extra-lean ground turkey
- 1½ teaspoons olive oil

SAUCE

- 2 tablespoons olive oil
- 2 tablespoons all-purpose flour
- 1½ cups reduced-sodium beef broth
- 1 tablespoon low-sodium Worcestershire sauce
- 1 tablespoon A.1. steak sauce
- 1 can (4 ounces) sliced mushrooms, drained

1. In a large bowl, combine ⅓ cup bread crumbs, onion, Worcestershire sauce, steak sauce, garlic and the seasonings. Add turkey; mix lightly but thoroughly. Shape into four ½-in.-thick oval patties. Place the remaining bread crumbs in a shallow bowl. Press patties into crumbs, patting to help coating adhere.

2. In a large nonstick skillet coated with cooking spray, heat 1½ teaspoons oil over medium heat. Add the patties; cook 3-4 minutes on each side or until a thermometer reads 165°. Remove from pan.

3. In same pan, heat 2 tablespoons oil over medium heat. Stir in flour until smooth; gradually whisk in the broth, Worcestershire sauce and steak sauce. Bring to a boil, stirring constantly; cook and stir 1-2 minutes or until thickened. Stir in the mushrooms. Return patties to the pan. Reduce heat; simmer, covered, 2-3 minutes or until heated through.

TURKEY SALISBURY STEAKS

CHICKEN & GARLIC
WITH FRESH HERBS

FAST FIX
CHICKEN & GARLIC WITH FRESH HERBS

The key to this savory chicken is the combination of garlic and fresh rosemary and thyme. I like to serve it with mashed potatoes or Italian bread.

—JAN VALDEZ LOMBARD, IL

START TO FINISH: 30 MIN.
MAKES: 6 SERVINGS

- 6 boneless skinless chicken thighs (about 1½ pounds)
- ½ teaspoon salt
- ¼ teaspoon pepper
- 1 tablespoon olive oil
- 10 garlic cloves, peeled and halved
- 2 tablespoons brandy or chicken stock
- 1 cup chicken stock
- 1 teaspoon minced fresh rosemary or ¼ teaspoon dried rosemary, crushed
- ½ teaspoon minced fresh thyme or ⅛ teaspoon dried thyme
- 1 tablespoon minced fresh chives

1. Sprinkle chicken with salt and pepper. In a large skillet, heat oil over medium-high heat. Brown chicken on both sides. Remove from pan.
2. Remove skillet from heat; add halved garlic cloves and brandy. Return to heat; cook and stir over medium heat 1-2 minutes or until liquid is almost evaporated.
3. Stir in the stock, rosemary and thyme; return chicken to pan. Bring to a boil. Reduce heat; simmer, uncovered, 6-8 minutes or until a thermometer reads 170°. Sprinkle with chives.

CHICKEN SAUSAGES
WITH POLENTA

CHICKEN SAUSAGES WITH POLENTA

I get a kick out of serving this dish—everyone is always on time for dinner when they know it's on the menu.

—ANGELA SPENGLER TAMPA, FL

START TO FINISH: 30 MIN.
MAKES: 6 SERVINGS

- 4 teaspoons olive oil, divided
- 1 tube (1 pound) polenta, cut into ½-inch slices
- 1 each medium green, sweet red and yellow peppers, thinly sliced
- 1 medium onion, thinly sliced
- 1 package (12 ounces) fully cooked Italian chicken sausage links, thinly sliced
- ¼ cup grated Parmesan cheese
- 1 tablespoon minced fresh basil

1. In a large nonstick skillet, heat 2 teaspoons oil over medium heat. Add the polenta; cook 9-11 minutes on each side or until golden brown. Keep warm.

2. Meanwhile, in another large skillet, heat remaining oil over medium-high heat. Add the peppers and onion; cook and stir until tender. Remove from pan.

3. Add sausages to same pan; cook and stir 4-5 minutes or until browned. Return pepper mixture to pan; heat through. Serve with polenta; sprinkle with cheese and basil.

MAKE IT SIZZLE

Chicken sausage, a versatile ingredient, comes in a variety of flavors. Want to try something different from the Italian-flavored chicken sausage called for in this recipe? Feel free to swap in apple- or chipotle-flavored chicken sausage instead. As an added benefit, chicken sausage has fewer calories and less sodium than pork sausage.

SOUTHWEST TURKEY LETTUCE WRAPS

If you're tired of the same old taco routine, give these a try. I tweaked a friend's recipe to suit our tastes and my family's loved it since. It's yummy, a breeze to make and fun to eat.

—ALLY BILLHORN WILTON, IA

START TO FINISH: 25 MIN.
MAKES: 6 SERVINGS

- 2 pounds extra-lean ground turkey
- 1 small onion, finely chopped
- 1 can (15 ounces) tomato sauce
- 2 tablespoons chili powder
- ½ teaspoon salt
- ¾ teaspoon ground cumin
- ½ teaspoon pepper
- 18 Bibb or iceberg lettuce leaves
- ¾ cup shredded cheddar cheese
  Optional toppings: sour cream, salsa and guacamole

1. In a large skillet, cook turkey and onion over medium-high heat 8-10 minutes or until turkey is no longer pink and onion is tender, breaking up turkey into crumbles.

2. Stir in the tomato sauce and seasonings. Bring to a boil. Reduce heat; simmer, covered, 10-12 minutes to allow flavors to blend. Serve in lettuce leaves with cheese and toppings as desired.

FREEZE OPTION *Freeze cooled meat mixture in freezer containers. To use, partially thaw in refrigerator overnight. Heat through in a saucepan, stirring occasionally and adding a little water if necessary.*

TUSCAN CHICKEN AND BEANS

TUSCAN CHICKEN AND BEANS

Who doesn't like flavorful meals that are also quick and easy? The rosemary and white beans are classic partners in this rustic Italian dish.

—MARIE RIZZIO INTERLOCHEN, MI

START TO FINISH: 30 MIN.
MAKES: 4 SERVINGS

- 1 pound boneless skinless chicken breasts, cut into ¾-inch pieces
- 2 teaspoons minced fresh rosemary or ½ teaspoon dried rosemary
- ¼ teaspoon salt
- ¼ teaspoon coarsely ground pepper
- 1 cup reduced-sodium chicken broth
- 2 tablespoons sun-dried tomatoes (not packed in oil), chopped
- 1 can (15½ ounces) white kidney or cannellini beans, rinsed and drained

1. In a small bowl, combine chicken, rosemary, salt and pepper. In a large nonstick skillet coated with cooking spray, cook the chicken over medium heat until browned.

2. Stir in the broth and tomatoes. Bring to a boil. Reduce heat; simmer, uncovered, for 3-5 minutes or until chicken juices run clear. Add beans; heat through.

**BROCCOLI, RICE AND
SAUSAGE DINNER,
PAGE 39**

47

44

47

PORK

Simple doesn't have to mean boring! These **tasty entrees** prove you need just a few ingredients to create the latest **family favorite.** Let **everyday ingredients star** at the table tonight: bacon, ham and sausage.

**HAM AND PEA
PASTA ALFREDO**

ZUCCHINI & SAUSAGE STOVETOP CASSEROLE

Gather zucchini from your garden or farm stand and start cooking. My family goes wild for this wholesome casserole. We like our zucchini grated, not sliced.

—**LEANN GRAY** TAYLORSVILLE, UT

START TO FINISH: 30 MIN.
MAKES: 6 SERVINGS

- 1 **pound bulk pork sausage**
- 1 **tablespoon canola oil**
- 3 **medium zucchini, thinly sliced**
- 1 **medium onion, chopped**
- 1 **can (14½ ounces) stewed tomatoes, cut up**
- 1 **package (8.8 ounces) ready-to-serve long grain rice**
- 1 **teaspoon prepared mustard**
- ½ **teaspoon garlic salt**
- ¼ **teaspoon pepper**
- 1 **cup (4 ounces) shredded sharp cheddar cheese**

1. In a large skillet, cook sausage over medium heat 5-7 minutes or until no longer pink, breaking into crumbles. Drain and remove sausage from pan.
2. In the same pan, heat oil over medium heat. Add zucchini and onion; cook and stir 5-7 minutes or until tender. Stir in the sausage, tomatoes, rice, mustard, garlic salt and pepper. Bring to a boil. Reduce heat; simmer, covered, 5 minutes to allow flavors to blend.
3. Remove from heat; sprinkle with cheese. Let stand, covered, 5 minutes or until cheese is melted.

HAM AND PEA PASTA ALFREDO

When I want a filling meal that even the kids enjoy, I toss ham and sugar snap peas with Romano cream sauce and pasta.

—**CR MONACHINO** KENMORE, NY

START TO FINISH: 25 MIN.
MAKES: 8 SERVINGS

- 1 **package (16 ounces) fettuccine**
- 2 **tablespoons butter**
- 1½ **pounds sliced fully cooked ham, cut into strips (about 5 cups)**
- 2 **cups fresh sugar snap peas**
- 2 **cups heavy whipping cream**
- ½ **cup grated Romano cheese**
- ¼ **teaspoon pepper**

1. Cook fettuccine according to package directions. Meanwhile, in a large skillet, heat the butter over medium heat. Add ham and peas; cook and stir 5 minutes. Stir in cream, cheese and pepper; bring to a boil. Reduce heat; simmer, uncovered, 1-2 minutes or until sauce is slightly thickened and peas are crisp-tender.
2. Drain fettuccine; add to skillet and toss to coat. Serve immediately.

RAVIOLI WITH SAUSAGE & TOMATO CREAM SAUCE

It tastes like you spent all day preparing these pasta pillows, but they are ready in just 30 minutes! Family and friends request my ravioli dish often.

—**CHERYL WEGENER** FESTUS, MO

START TO FINISH: 25 MIN.
MAKES: 4 SERVINGS

- 1 **package (9 ounces) refrigerated cheese ravioli**
- ¾ **pound bulk Italian sausage**
- 1 **jar (24 ounces) tomato basil pasta sauce**
- ½ **cup heavy whipping cream**
- 2 **bacon strips, cooked and crumbled**
- 2 **tablespoons grated Parmesan cheese**
  Minced fresh parsley

1. Cook ravioli according to package directions. Meanwhile, cook sausage in a large skillet over medium heat until no longer pink; drain. Stir in pasta sauce, cream and bacon. Bring to a boil; reduce the heat. Simmer, uncovered, for 2 minutes or until slightly thickened.
2. Drain ravioli; stir into sauce. Top with Parmesan cheese and parsley.

DID YOU KNOW?

Long grain rice and instant rice (which is precooked before packaging) require different amounts of liquid during cooking, so they can't be substituted measure-for-measure in recipes. Once prepared, however, you can use either kind of rice to fit your preference.

PORK SCALLOPINI WITH MUSHROOMS

This is a great at-home date night recipe. I add salt to season the meat and mushrooms, and then use reduced-sodium chicken broth for the sauce.

—**LANA DRAMSTAD** HAVRE, MT

START TO FINISH: 30 MIN.
MAKES: 4 SERVINGS

- 1 pork tenderloin (1 pound), cut into eight slices
- 1 teaspoon salt, divided
- ½ teaspoon pepper, divided
- 4 tablespoons butter, divided
- ½ pound sliced fresh mushrooms
- 2 celery ribs, sliced
- 1 cup reduced-sodium chicken broth
- ⅓ cup heavy whipping cream
- 3 tablespoons minced fresh parsley, divided
  Hot cooked egg noodles

1. Pound the pork slices with a meat mallet to ½-in. thickness; sprinkle with ½ teaspoon salt and ¼ teaspoon pepper. In a large skillet, heat 1 tablespoon butter over medium-high heat. Add the pork in batches; cook 2-3 minutes on each side or until pork is golden brown, using 1 tablespoon butter as needed. Remove; keep warm.

2. In the same pan, heat remaining butter over medium heat. Add the mushrooms, celery and remaining salt and pepper; cook and stir for 6-8 minutes or until tender. Add broth, stirring to loosen browned bits from pan. Bring to a boil; cook 5-6 minutes or until liquid is reduced to ⅔ cup.

3. Return the pork to pan. Stir in the cream and 2 tablespoons parsley; heat through. Serve with noodles; sprinkle with remaining parsley.

ZUCCHINI & SAUSAGE STOVETOP CASSEROLE

PORK SCALLOPINI WITH MUSHROOMS

ALMOND-CRUSTED CHOPS
WITH CIDER SAUCE

PUMPKIN &
SAUSAGE PENNE

FAST FIX

ALMOND-CRUSTED CHOPS WITH CIDER SAUCE

Finely ground almonds give pork chops a crunchy crust—and the cider sauce makes them tangy, creamy and sweet.
—**GLORIA BRADLEY** NAPERVILLE, IL

START TO FINISH: 20 MIN.
MAKES: 4 SERVINGS

- ½ **cup panko (Japanese) bread crumbs**
- ½ **cup ground almonds**
- ⅓ **cup all-purpose flour**
- ½ **teaspoon salt, divided**
- 2 **large eggs, beaten**
- 4 **boneless pork loin chops (¾ inch thick and 4 ounces each)**
- 3 **tablespoons olive oil**
- 1 **cup apple cider or juice**
- 4 **ounces cream cheese, cubed**
- 1 **tablespoon honey, optional**
  Minced chives

1. In a bowl, mix bread crumbs and almonds. In another bowl, mix flour and ¼ teaspoon salt. Place eggs in a separate shallow bowl. Dip pork chops in flour to coat both sides; shake off excess. Dip in egg, then in crumb mixture, patting to help coating adhere.

2. In a large skillet, heat the oil over medium heat. Add pork chops; cook 3-4 minutes on each side or until a thermometer reads 145°. Remove; keep warm. Wipe skillet clean.

3. In same skillet over medium heat, combine apple cider, cream cheese, remaining salt and, if desired, honey. Cook and stir 2 minutes. Serve with pork chops; sprinkle with chives.

FAST FIX

PUMPKIN & SAUSAGE PENNE

I once made this dish for my Italian father-in-law, who swears he'll eat pasta only with red sauce. He loved it!
—**KAREN CAMBIOTTI** STROUDSBURG, PA

START TO FINISH: 30 MIN.
MAKES: 2 SERVINGS

- ¾ **cup uncooked penne pasta**
- 2 **Italian sausage links, casings removed**
- ½ **cup chopped sweet onion**
- 1 **garlic clove, minced**
- 1 **teaspoon olive oil**
- ⅓ **cup white wine or chicken broth**
- 1 **bay leaf**
- ¾ **cup chicken broth**
- ⅓ **cup canned pumpkin**
- 3 **teaspoons minced fresh sage, divided**
- ⅛ **teaspoon each salt, pepper and ground cinnamon**
  Dash ground nutmeg
- 3 **tablespoons half-and-half cream**
- 2 **tablespoons shredded Romano cheese**

1. Cook pasta according to package directions. Meanwhile, in a large skillet, cook sausage over medium heat until no longer pink, breaking into crumbles. Remove with a slotted spoon; drain on paper towels. Discard drippings, reserving 1 teaspoon.

2. Cook and stir onion and garlic in the oil and reserved drippings over medium-high heat until tender. Add wine and bay leaf. Bring to a boil; cook until liquid is reduced by half. Stir in broth, pumpkin, 1½ teaspoons sage and remaining seasonings; cook 1 minute longer. Add the cream and sausage; heat through. Remove the bay leaf.

3. Drain pasta; transfer to a large bowl. Add sausage mixture; toss to coat. Sprinkle with the cheese and remaining sage.

BROCCOLI, RICE AND SAUSAGE DINNER

The first recipe my kids requested when they were on their own was my broccoli with sausage and rice dish. If fresh zucchini or summer squash is available, add them to the mix.
—**JOANN PARMENTIER** BRANCH, MI

START TO FINISH: 25 MIN.
MAKES: 6 SERVINGS

- 1 tablespoon canola oil
- 1 package (13 ounces) smoked turkey sausage, sliced
- 4 cups small fresh broccoli florets
- 2 cups water
- 1 can (14½ ounces) diced tomatoes, drained
- ¼ teaspoon seasoned salt
- ¼ teaspoon garlic powder
- ¼ teaspoon dried oregano
- 2 cups uncooked instant brown rice
- ½ cup shredded sharp cheddar cheese
  Sour cream and Louisiana-style hot sauce, optional

1. In a large skillet, heat the oil over medium-high heat. Add the sausage; cook and stir 2-3 minutes or until browned. Stir in broccoli; cook and stir 2 minutes longer.
2. Add the water, tomatoes and seasonings; bring to a boil. Stir in the rice. Reduce heat; simmer, covered, 5 minutes.
3. Remove from heat; stir the rice mixture and sprinkle with cheese. Let stand, covered, 5 minutes or until liquid is almost absorbed and cheese is melted. If desired, serve with sour cream and hot sauce.

BACON-SWISS PORK CHOPS

I'm always looking for quick recipes that are impressive enough to serve company. These pork chops smothered in bacon and Swiss cheese certainly deliver.
—**KEITH MILLER** FORT GRATIOT, MI

START TO FINISH: 25 MIN.
MAKES: 4 SERVINGS

- 2 bacon strips, chopped
- 1 medium onion, chopped
- 4 boneless pork loin chops (4 ounces each)
- ½ teaspoon garlic powder
- ¼ teaspoon salt
- 2 slices reduced-fat Swiss cheese, halved

1. In a nonstick skillet coated with cooking spray, cook bacon and onion over medium heat until bacon is crisp, stirring occasionally. Drain on paper towels; discard drippings.
2. Sprinkle pork chops with garlic powder and salt. Add pork chops to same pan; cook over medium heat 3-4 minutes on each side or until a thermometer reads 145°. Top the pork with bacon mixture and cheese. Cook, covered, on low heat for 1-2 minutes or until cheese is melted. Let stand 5 minutes before serving.

ITALIAN CHOPS WITH PASTA

Thanks to an Italian makeover, this pork is perfection in a skillet. Tender chops, red wine, fire-roasted tomatoes and penne pasta make a luscious, complete meal in minutes.
—***TASTE OF HOME*** TEST KITCHEN

START TO FINISH: 30 MIN.
MAKES: 4 SERVINGS

- 4 bone-in pork loin chops (8 ounces each)
- ½ teaspoon salt
- ½ teaspoon pepper
- 1 tablespoon olive oil
- 1 medium green pepper, chopped
- 1 medium red onion, chopped
- 3 garlic cloves, minced
- ⅓ cup dry red wine or chicken broth
- 2 cans (14½ ounces each) fire-roasted diced tomatoes, undrained
- 1½ teaspoons Italian seasoning
  Hot cooked penne pasta
  Shredded Parmesan cheese, optional

1. Sprinkle pork chops with salt and pepper. Brown chops in oil in a large skillet. Remove and keep warm. Saute green pepper and onion in the same skillet until crisp-tender. Add garlic; cook 1 minute longer.
2. Add the wine, stirring to loosen browned bits from pan. Bring to a boil; cook until liquid is almost evaporated. Add tomatoes and Italian seasoning. Cook and stir for 2-3 minutes or until sauce is slightly thickened.
3. Return chops to the skillet. Cover and simmer for 3-5 minutes or until a thermometer reads 145°. Let stand for 5 minutes before serving. Serve with pasta. Sprinkle with cheese if desired.

BROCCOLI, RICE AND SAUSAGE DINNER

FAST FIX ▶

SOUTHWEST SKILLET CHOPS

This is one of my go-to meals because I usually have all the ingredients on hand. I personally can't get enough of the same-dish corn relish.

—LINDA CIFUENTES MAHOMET, IL

START TO FINISH: 25 MIN.
MAKES: 4 SERVINGS

- 4 **boneless pork loin chops (6 ounces each)**
- ¾ **teaspoon salt**
- ¼ **teaspoon pepper**
- 2 **tablespoons butter, divided**
- 1 **tablespoon olive oil**
- ½ **small red onion, sliced**
- 1 **jalapeno pepper, seeded and finely chopped**
- ½ **cup frozen corn, thawed**
- 3 **tablespoons lime juice**
- ¼ **cup sliced ripe olives or green olives with pimientos, optional**

1. Sprinkle the pork chops with salt and pepper. In a large skillet, heat 1 tablespoon butter and oil over medium-high heat. Brown pork chops on both sides. Remove from pan.

2. In the same skillet, heat remaining butter. Add the onion and jalapeno; cook and stir 2-3 minutes or until tender. Return chops to skillet. Add corn, lime juice and, if desired, olives; cook, covered, 4-6 minutes or until a thermometer inserted in pork reads 145°. Let dish stand for 5 minutes before serving.

NOTE *Wear disposable gloves when cutting hot peppers; the oils can burn skin. Avoid touching your face.*

SOUTHWEST SKILLET CHOPS

PORK SCHNITZEL WITH DILL SAUCE

Schnitzel is one of my husband's favorites. It reminds him of his German roots, and I like that it's easy to make for a group.
—JOYCE FOLKER PARAOWAN, UT

PREP: 20 MIN. • **COOK:** 20 MIN.
MAKES: 6 SERVINGS

- ½ cup all-purpose flour
- 2 teaspoons seasoned salt
- ½ teaspoon pepper
- 2 large eggs
- ¼ cup 2% milk
- 1½ cups dry bread crumbs
- 2 teaspoons paprika
- 6 pork sirloin cutlets (4 ounces each)
- 6 tablespoons canola oil

DILL SAUCE
- 2 tablespoons all-purpose flour
- 1½ cups chicken broth, divided
- 1 cup (8 ounces) sour cream
- ½ teaspoon dill weed

1. In a shallow bowl, mix the flour, seasoned salt and pepper. In a second shallow bowl, whisk eggs and milk until blended. In a third bowl, mix bread crumbs and paprika.

2. Pound pork cutlets with a meat mallet to ¼-in. thickness. Dip cutlets in flour mixture to coat both sides; shake off excess. Dip in egg mixture, then in crumb mixture, patting to help coating adhere.

3. In a large skillet, heat oil over medium heat. Add pork in batches; cook 2-3 minutes on each side or until golden brown. Remove to a serving plate; keep warm. Wipe skillet clean if necessary.

4. In a small bowl, whisk flour and broth until smooth; add to same skillet. Bring to a boil, stirring constantly; cook and stir 2 minutes or until thickened.

5. Reduce heat to low. Stir in sour cream and dill; heat through (do not boil). Serve with pork.

FAST FIX
RIGATONI WITH SAUSAGE & PEAS

With a meaty tomato sauce and tangy goat cheese, this weeknight wonder is my version of comfort food. You just want to have bowl after bowl.
—LIZZIE MUNRO BROOKLYN, NY

START TO FINISH: 30 MIN.
MAKES: 6 SERVINGS

- 12 ounces uncooked rigatoni or large tube pasta
- 1 pound bulk Italian sausage
- 4 garlic cloves, minced
- ¼ cup tomato paste
- 1 can (28 ounces) crushed tomatoes
- ½ teaspoon dried basil
- ¼ to ½ teaspoon crushed red pepper flakes
- 1½ cups frozen peas
- ½ cup heavy whipping cream
- ½ cup crumbled goat or feta cheese
  Thinly sliced fresh basil, optional

1. Cook rigatoni according to the package directions.

2. Meanwhile, in a Dutch oven, cook the sausage over medium heat 6-8 minutes or until no longer pink, breaking into crumbles. Add the garlic; cook 1 minute longer. Drain. Add tomato paste; cook and stir 2-3 minutes or until meat is coated. Stir in the tomatoes, dried basil and pepper flakes; bring to a boil. Reduce heat; simmer, uncovered, 10-15 minutes or until thickened, stirring occasionally.

3. Drain rigatoni; stir into sausage mixture. Add peas and cream; heat through. Top with the cheese and, if desired, fresh basil.

RIGATONI WITH SAUSAGE & PEAS

APRICOT PORK MEDALLIONS

In our house, there's nothing we love more than a great pork dish for supper, and this recipe is up there with the best of them. I find that apricot preserves give pork just the right amount of sweetness without being overwhelming.
—**CRYSTAL JO BRUNS** ILIFF, CO

START TO FINISH: 20 MIN.
MAKES: 4 SERVINGS

- 1 pork tenderloin (1 pound), cut into eight slices
- 1 tablespoon plus 1 teaspoon butter, divided
- ½ cup apricot preserves
- 2 green onions, sliced
- 1 tablespoon cider vinegar
- ¼ teaspoon ground mustard

1. Pound pork slices with a meat mallet to ½-in. thickness. In a large skillet, heat 1 tablespoon butter over medium heat. Brown pork on each side. Remove the pork from pan, reserving drippings.
2. Add the preserves, green onions, vinegar, mustard and remaining butter to the pan; bring just to a boil, stirring to loosen browned bits from pan. Reduce heat; simmer, covered, 3-4 minutes to allow flavors to blend.
3. Return the pork to pan; cook until pork is tender. Let stand 5 minutes before serving.

BISTRO HERB-RUBBED PORK TENDERLOIN

A mouthwatering rub featuring fresh tarragon, thyme and rosemary releases rich, bold flavor as this pork entree sizzles. Served with a delectable thickened sauce, it's crazy good!
—**NAYLET LAROCHELLE** MIAMI, FL

PREP: 20 MIN. + MARINATING • **COOK:** 20 MIN.
MAKES: 4 SERVINGS

- 3 tablespoons minced fresh tarragon
- 2 tablespoons minced fresh thyme
- 1 tablespoon minced fresh rosemary
- 2 garlic cloves, minced
- 2 teaspoons smoked paprika
- 1 teaspoon kosher salt
- ¼ teaspoon coarsely ground pepper
- 6 tablespoons olive oil, divided
- 1 pork tenderloin (1 pound), cut into 12 slices
- 1 tablespoon all-purpose flour
- ½ cup beef broth
- 2 tablespoons minced fresh chives

1. In a small bowl, combine tarragon, thyme, rosemary, garlic, paprika, salt, pepper and 4 tablespoons oil. Flatten pork slices to ¼-in. thickness. Rub slices with herb mixture; cover and refrigerate 15 minutes.
2. In a large skillet, cook the pork in the remaining oil in batches over medium-high heat 1-2 minutes on each side or until browned. Remove and keep warm.
3. Stir flour into pan until blended; gradually add broth. Bring to a boil; cook and stir 2 minutes or until thickened. Serve with the pork and sprinkle with chives.

CREAMY SAUSAGE-MUSHROOM RIGATONI

When visiting Rome, we enjoyed an amazing dinner at a restaurant near the Pantheon. It lasted three hours! The restaurant is now gone, but its memory lives on in this tasty little dish.
—**BARBARA ROOZROKH** BROOKFIELD, WI

START TO FINISH: 30 MIN.
MAKES: 6 SERVINGS

- 1 package (16 ounces) rigatoni
- 1 pound bulk Italian sausage
- 2 teaspoons butter
- 1 pound sliced fresh mushrooms
- 2 garlic cloves, minced
- ½ teaspoon salt
- ¼ teaspoon pepper
- 2 cups heavy whipping cream
  Minced fresh parsley, optional

1. Cook rigatoni according to the package directions.
2. Meanwhile, in a large skillet, cook the sausage over medium heat 4-6 minutes or until no longer pink, breaking into crumbles; drain and remove sausage from pan.
3. In same skillet, heat butter over medium heat. Add the mushrooms, garlic, salt and pepper; cook, covered, 4 minutes, stirring occasionally. Uncover; cook and stir 2-3 minutes or until mushrooms are tender and liquid is evaporated.
4. Stir in the cream; bring to a boil. Reduce the heat; cook, uncovered, 8-10 minutes or until slightly thickened. Return the sausage to skillet; heat through. Drain pasta; serve with the sauce. If desired, sprinkle with parsley.

PORK VEGETABLE SKILLET

Eggplant is wonderful with pork and other veggies. Pick one that has firm, smooth skin and no soft spots. Use within one or two days of purchase: it's very perishable.
—*TASTE OF HOME* TEST KITCHEN

START TO FINISH: 30 MIN.
MAKES: 6 SERVINGS

- 1½ pounds boneless pork loin chops, cubed
- 2 tablespoons olive oil, divided
- 3 cups cubed eggplant
- 1 medium zucchini, chopped
- 1 medium onion, chopped
- 1 cup fresh baby carrots, cut in half lengthwise
- 1 can (14½ ounces) diced tomatoes with garlic and onion, undrained
- 1 can (10¾ ounces) condensed cream of celery soup, undiluted
- 1 cup (4 ounces) sharp shredded cheddar cheese
- ¼ cup water
- ½ teaspoon salt
- ½ teaspoon dried oregano
- ½ teaspoon dried marjoram
  Hot cooked fettuccine

1. Cook pork in a large skillet over medium heat in 1 tablespoon oil until browned; remove and keep warm.
2. In the same skillet, saute the eggplant, zucchini, onion and carrots in remaining oil until tender. Stir in the tomatoes, soup, cheese, water, salt and seasonings; add pork. Bring to a boil. Reduce heat; simmer, uncovered, for 5 minutes. Serve with fettuccine.

SKILLET PORK CHOPS
WITH APPLES & ONION

⑤ INGREDIENTS FAST FIX

SKILLET PORK CHOPS WITH APPLES & ONION

Simple recipes that land on the table fast are a lifesaver some days. I serve skillet pork chops with veggies and, when there's more time, corn bread stuffing.

—TRACEY KARST PONDERAY, ID

START TO FINISH: 20 MIN.
MAKES: 4 SERVINGS

- 4 **boneless pork loin chops (6 ounces each)**
- 3 **medium apples, cut into wedges**
- 1 **large onion, cut into thin wedges**
- ¼ **cup water**
- ⅓ **cup balsamic vinaigrette**
- ½ **teaspoon salt**
- ¼ **teaspoon pepper**

1. Place a large nonstick skillet over medium heat; brown pork chops on both sides, about 4 minutes. Remove from pan.

2. In the same skillet, combine the apples, onion and water. Place pork chops over apple mixture; drizzle chops with vinaigrette. Sprinkle with salt and pepper. Reduce heat; simmer, covered, for 3-5 minutes or until a thermometer inserted in the pork chops reads 145°.

BLT SKILLET

This weeknight meal is fast and, with its chunks of bacon and tomato, reminiscent of a BLT. Whole wheat linguine gives the dish a little extra texture and body.

—EDRIE O'BRIEN DENVER, CO

START TO FINISH: 25 MIN.
MAKES: 2 SERVINGS

- 4 ounces uncooked whole wheat linguine
- 4 bacon strips, cut into 1½-inch pieces
- 1 plum tomato, cut into 1-inch pieces
- 1 garlic clove, minced
- 1½ teaspoons lemon juice
- ¼ teaspoon salt
- ¼ teaspoon pepper
- 2 tablespoons grated Parmesan cheese
- 1 tablespoon minced fresh parsley

1. Cook linguine according to the package directions. Meanwhile, in a large skillet, cook the bacon over medium heat until crisp. Remove to paper towels; drain bacon, reserving 1 teaspoon drippings.

2. In the drippings, saute tomato and garlic for 1-2 minutes or until heated through. Stir in bacon, lemon juice, salt and pepper.

3. Drain linguine; add to the skillet. Sprinkle with cheese and parsley; toss to coat.

BLT SKILLET

BREADED PORK TENDERLOIN

My teenage daughter is slightly picky about food, but here's one entree she loves. Drizzle ranch dressing or barbecue sauce on top of the tenderloin.

—DONNA CARNEY NEW LEXINGTON, OH

START TO FINISH: 30 MIN.
MAKES: 4 SERVINGS

- 1 pork tenderloin (1 pound)
- ⅓ cup all-purpose flour
- ⅓ cup corn bread/muffin mix
- ½ teaspoon salt
- ¼ teaspoon pepper
- 1 large egg, beaten
- 4 tablespoons canola oil, divided
  Ranch or barbecue sauce, optional

1. Cut the pork crosswise into ½-in. slices. In a shallow bowl, mix flour, muffin mix, salt and pepper. Place egg in a separate shallow bowl. Dip pork in egg, then in flour mixture, patting to help coating adhere.

2. In a large skillet, heat 2 tablespoons oil over medium heat. Add half of the pork; cook 3-4 minutes on each side or until a thermometer reads 145°. Drain on paper towels. Wipe skillet clean; repeat with remaining oil and pork. If desired, serve with sauce.

SUMMER CARBONARA

Basil and bacon make sensational partners. I add a simple spring mix salad with balsamic dressing and a glass of Chardonnay or iced tea.

—CATHY DUDDERAR LEXINGTON, KY

PREP: 25 MIN. • **COOK:** 10 MIN.
MAKES: 6 SERVINGS

- 1 package (16 ounces) spaghetti
- 1 large sweet onion, finely chopped
- 1 medium yellow summer squash, finely chopped
- 1 medium zucchini, finely chopped
- 2 garlic cloves, minced
- 2 tablespoons olive oil
- 4 plum tomatoes, seeded and chopped
- 2 large eggs, beaten
- 1 cup grated Parmesan cheese
- 12 bacon strips, cooked and crumbled
- ¼ cup fresh basil leaves, thinly sliced

- 1 teaspoon minced fresh oregano or ½ teaspoon dried oregano
- ½ teaspoon salt
- ¼ teaspoon pepper

1. Cook spaghetti according to the package directions. Meanwhile, in a large skillet, saute the onion, squash, zucchini and garlic in oil until tender. Add tomatoes; heat through. Remove and keep warm.

2. Reduce heat to low; add the eggs to the skillet. Cook and stir until the egg mixture coats a metal spoon and reaches 160° (mixture will look like a soft frothy egg). Drain spaghetti and place in a bowl. Add eggs; toss to coat. Add the vegetable mixture, cheese, bacon, basil, oregano, salt and pepper; toss gently to coat.

PORK AND WAFFLES WITH MAPLE-PEAR TOPPING

Maple syrup and Dijon mustard come through beautifully in these upscale, crowd-pleasing waffles.

—*TASTE OF HOME* TEST KITCHEN

START TO FINISH: 25 MIN.
MAKES: 4 SERVINGS

- ½ cup seasoned bread crumbs
- 1 teaspoon dried thyme
- 1 pork tenderloin (1 pound), cut into 12 slices
- 2 tablespoons olive oil
- 2 medium pears, thinly sliced
- ½ cup maple syrup
- 2 tablespoons Dijon mustard
- ½ teaspoon salt
- 8 frozen waffles, toasted
- 2 tablespoons minced chives

1. In a large resealable plastic bag, combine bread crumbs and thyme. Add pork, a few pieces at a time, and shake to coat. In a large skillet, cook pork in oil in batches over medium heat for 2-4 minutes on each side or until tender. Remove from the pan and keep warm.

2. Add the pears, syrup, mustard and salt to the skillet; cook and stir for 1-2 minutes or until pears are tender. Serve pork slices and pear mixture over waffles. Sprinkle with chives.

RASPBERRY PORK MEDALLIONS

Pork served with a luscious raspberry glaze is fancy enough for company. We bring it to the table with wild rice pilaf and steamed veggies.

—**TRISHA KRUSE** EAGLE, ID

START TO FINISH: 25 MIN.
MAKES: 4 SERVINGS

- 1 **pork tenderloin (1 pound)**
- 1 **tablespoon canola oil**
- 2 **tablespoons reduced-sodium soy sauce**
- 1 **garlic clove, minced**
- ½ **teaspoon ground ginger**
- 1 **cup fresh raspberries**
- 2 **tablespoons seedless raspberry spreadable fruit**
- 2 **teaspoons minced fresh basil**
- ½ **teaspoon minced fresh mint, optional**

1. Cut tenderloin crosswise into eight slices; pound each with a meat mallet to ½-in. thickness. In a large skillet, heat oil over medium-high heat. Add pork; cook 3-4 minutes on each side or until thermometer in pork reads 145°. Remove from pan; keep warm.
2. Reduce heat to medium-low; add soy sauce, garlic and ginger to pan, stirring to loosen browned bits from pan. Add raspberries, spreadable fruit, basil and, if desired, mint; cook and stir 2-3 minutes or until slightly thickened. Serve with the pork.

HOW TO CHOP BASIL

To quickly chop a lot of basil, stack several leaves and roll them into a tight tube. Slice the leaves widthwise into narrow pieces to create long thin strips. If you're mincing the basil, chop the strips again.

RASPBERRY PORK MEDALLIONS

PRETTY PENNE HAM SKILLET

FAST FIX

PRETTY PENNE HAM SKILLET

I'm a busy nurse, so fast meals are a must. This pasta is a tasty change of pace from potato-ham casseroles.

—**KATHY STEPHAN** WEST SENECA, NY

START TO FINISH: 30 MIN.
MAKES: 6 SERVINGS

- 1 **package (16 ounces) penne pasta**
- ¼ **cup olive oil**
- 3 **tablespoons butter**
- 3 **cups cubed fully cooked ham**
- 1 **large sweet red pepper, finely chopped**
- 1 **medium onion, chopped**
- 2 **garlic cloves, minced**
- ¼ **cup minced fresh parsley**
- 1½ **teaspoons minced fresh basil or ½ teaspoon dried basil**
- 1½ **teaspoons minced fresh oregano or ½ teaspoon dried oregano**
- 1 **can (14½ ounces) chicken broth**
- 1 **tablespoon lemon juice**
- ½ **cup shredded Parmesan cheese**

1. Cook pasta according to package directions; drain. Meanwhile, in a large skillet, heat the oil and butter over medium-high heat. Add ham, red pepper and onion; cook and stir 4-6 minutes or until ham is browned and vegetables are tender. Add garlic and herbs; cook 1-2 minutes longer.
2. Stir in the broth and lemon juice. Bring to a boil. Reduce heat; simmer, uncovered, 10-15 minutes or until liquid is reduced by half. Add pasta; toss to combine. Sprinkle with cheese.

MAKE IT SIZZLE

We loved this recipe! Definitely quick and easy. The only changes that I made were to use tri-color penne and to double the lemon juice. I served it with Greek salad and garlic bread.

—**KATLAYDEE3** TASTEOFHOME.COM

ITALIAN SAUSAGE WITH ARTICHOKES AND FETA

ITALIAN SAUSAGE WITH ARTICHOKES AND FETA

To impress the guests, we serve Italian sausage and artichoke hearts with pasta. It tastes like a gourmet masterpiece, and it's equally good with rice or potatoes.
—AYSHA SCHURMAN AMMON, ID

START TO FINISH: 25 MIN.
MAKES: 4 SERVINGS

- 1 pound bulk Italian sausage
- 1 small red onion, finely chopped
- 1 garlic clove, minced
- 1 jar (7½ ounces) marinated quartered artichoke hearts, drained and coarsely chopped
- ½ cup tomato sauce
- ¼ cup dry red wine or chicken broth
- ½ teaspoon Italian seasoning
- ½ cup crumbled feta cheese
  Minced fresh parsley, optional
  Hot cooked gemelli or spiral pasta

1. In a skillet, cook sausage, onion and garlic over medium heat 6-8 minutes or until sausage is no longer pink and onion is tender, breaking up sausage into crumbles; drain.
2. Stir in artichoke hearts, tomato sauce, wine and Italian seasoning; heat through. Gently stir in cheese. If desired, sprinkle with parsley. Serve with pasta.

FREEZE OPTION *Freeze the cooled sausage mixture in freezer containers. To use, partially thaw in refrigerator overnight. Place sausage mixture in a saucepan; heat through, stirring occasionally and adding a little broth or water if necessary.*

CHEESE & MUSHROOM SKILLET PIZZA

This Italian skillet toss is an awesome way to use up extra spaghetti sauce. It fits right in on Friday pizza night.
—CLARE BUTLER LITTLE ELM, TX

START TO FINISH: 30 MIN.
MAKES: 4 SLICES

- 1 cup all-purpose flour
- 2 teaspoons baking powder
- 1 teaspoon dried oregano
- ½ teaspoon salt
- 6 tablespoons water

- 2 tablespoons plus 1 teaspoon olive oil, divided
- ½ cup pizza sauce
- 25 slices pepperoni
- 1 jar (4½ ounces) sliced mushrooms, drained
- 1 can (2¼ ounces) sliced ripe olives, drained
- 1 cup (4 ounces) shredded part-skim mozzarella cheese

1. Preheat broiler. In a small bowl, whisk the flour, baking powder, oregano and salt. Stir in water and 2 tablespoons oil to form a soft dough. Turn onto a floured surface; knead 6-8 times. Roll into a 12-in. circle.
2. Brush bottom of a 12-in. ovenproof skillet with remaining oil; place over medium-high heat. Transfer dough to pan; cook 2-3 minutes on each side or until golden brown. Remove from heat. Spread with pizza sauce; top with pepperoni, mushrooms, olives and cheese.
3. Broil 3-4 in. from heat 3-5 minutes or until cheese is melted.

PARMESAN PORK CUTLETS

The aroma of the cooking cutlets makes my kids eager to come to the dinner table.
—JULIE AHERN WAUKEGAN, IL

PREP: 25 MIN. • **COOK:** 15 MIN.
MAKES: 4 SERVINGS

- 1 pork tenderloin (1 pound)
- ⅓ cup all-purpose flour
- 2 large eggs, lightly beaten
- 1 cup dry bread crumbs
- ¼ cup grated Parmesan cheese
- 1 teaspoon salt
- ¼ cup olive oil
  Lemon wedges

1. Cut the pork diagonally into eight slices; pound each to ¼-in. thickness. Place the flour and eggs in separate shallow bowls. In another shallow bowl, combine the bread crumbs, cheese and salt. Dip pork in the flour, eggs, then bread crumb mixture.
2. In a large skillet, cook the pork in oil in batches over medium heat for 2-3 minutes on each side or until crisp and meat juices run clear. Remove and keep warm. Serve with lemon wedges.

SMOKY SAUSAGE & PEPPER SKILLET

SMOKY SAUSAGE & PEPPER SKILLET

My family loves this combination of sausage, green peppers and onions. It's a very popular birthday meal request!
—CELINDA KULP HUMMELSTOWN, PA

START TO FINISH: 30 MIN.
MAKES: 4 SERVINGS

- 1 pound smoked sausage, sliced
- 2 large green peppers, thinly sliced
- 1 medium onion, thinly sliced
- 1 garlic clove, minced
- 4 teaspoons cornstarch
- 2 cups whole milk
- ¼ cup minced fresh parsley
- ¾ teaspoon dried marjoram
- ½ teaspoon pepper
- ½ cup shredded Parmesan cheese
  Hot cooked rice or pasta

1. In a large skillet, brown sausage over medium heat. Remove with a slotted spoon; drain on paper towels.
2. Add the green peppers and onion to same skillet; cook and stir until vegetables are crisp-tender. Add the garlic; cook 1 minute longer. In a small bowl, mix cornstarch, milk, parsley, marjoram and pepper until blended; stir into the pan. Bring to a boil; cook and stir 2 minutes or until the sauce is thickened.
3. Return the sausage to pan; heat through. Stir in cheese until blended. Serve with rice.

**PAN-ROASTED SALMON
WITH CHERRY TOMATOES,
PAGE 56**

59

57

51

FISH & SEAFOOD

Set sail on a new eating adventure—these main dishes offer **loads of flavor.** Whether you're in the mood for scallops, mahi mahi, salmon or shrimp, you can't go adrift when plating up **enticing, winning recipes.**

**MAHI MAHI &
VEGGIE SKILLET**

MAHI MAHI &
VEGGIE SKILLET

Cooking mahi mahi and ratatouille may seem complex, but I've developed a skillet recipe that brings out the wow factor without the worry.

—**SOLOMON WANG** ARLINGTON, TX

START TO FINISH: 30 MIN.
MAKES: 4 SERVINGS

- 3 tablespoons olive oil, divided
- 4 mahi mahi or salmon fillets (6 ounces each)
- 3 medium sweet red peppers, cut into thick strips
- ½ pound sliced baby portobello mushrooms
- 1 large sweet onion, cut into thick rings and separated
- ⅓ cup lemon juice
- ¾ teaspoon salt, divided
- ½ teaspoon pepper
- ¼ cup minced fresh chives
- ⅓ cup pine nuts, optional

1. In a large skillet, heat 2 tablespoons oil over medium-high heat. Add fillets; cook 4-5 minutes on each side or until the fish just begins to flake easily with a fork. Remove from pan.

2. Add the remaining oil, peppers, mushrooms, onion, lemon juice and ¼ teaspoon salt. Cook, covered, over medium heat 6-8 minutes or until the vegetables are tender, stirring the mixture occasionally.

3. Place fish over vegetables; sprinkle with pepper and remaining salt. Cook, covered, 2 minutes longer or until heated through. Sprinkle with the chives and, if desired, the pine nuts before serving.

**STEAMED MUSSELS
WITH PEPPERS**

STEAMED MUSSELS WITH PEPPERS

Use the French bread to soak up the deliciously seasoned broth. If you like your food with more heat, throw in the jalapeno seeds.
—*TASTE OF HOME* TEST KITCHEN

PREP: 30 MIN. • **COOK:** 10 MIN.
MAKES: 4 SERVINGS

- 2 pounds fresh mussels, scrubbed and beards removed
- 1 jalapeno pepper, seeded and chopped
- 2 tablespoons olive oil
- 3 garlic cloves, minced
- 1 bottle (8 ounces) clam juice
- ½ cup white wine or additional clam juice
- ⅓ cup chopped sweet red pepper
- 3 green onions, sliced
- ½ teaspoon dried oregano
- 1 bay leaf
- 2 tablespoons minced fresh parsley
- ¼ teaspoon salt
- ¼ teaspoon pepper
  French bread baguette, sliced, optional

1. Tap mussels; discard any that do not close. Set aside. In a large skillet, saute jalapeno in oil until tender. Add garlic; cook 1 minute longer. Stir in the clam juice, wine, red pepper, green onions, oregano and bay leaf.
2. Bring to a boil. Reduce heat; add the mussels. Cover and simmer for 5-6 minutes or until the mussels open. Discard bay leaf and any unopened mussels. Sprinkle with parsley, salt and pepper. Serve with the baguette slices if desired.
STEAMED CLAMS WITH PEPPERS *Substitute clams for the mussels.*
NOTE *Wear disposable gloves when cutting hot peppers; the oils can burn skin. Avoid touching your face.*

LEMON & DILL SHRIMP SANDWICHES

FAST FIX
LEMON & DILL SHRIMP SANDWICHES

Our family took a once-in-a-lifetime trip to Norway, where we got to eat incredible shrimp sandwiches like these. The crispier the bread crust, the better.
—**MONICA KOLVA** MILLVILLE, NJ

START TO FINISH: 20 MIN.
MAKES: 4 SERVINGS

- 4 hoagie buns, split
- 1 tablespoon butter
- 1 pound uncooked shrimp (41-50 per pound), peeled and deveined
- ½ cup mayonnaise
- 2 tablespoons lemon juice
- 4 teaspoons snipped fresh dill or 1¼ teaspoons dill weed
- ½ teaspoon salt
- ¼ teaspoon pepper
  Shredded lettuce and sliced tomato, optional

1. Hollow out bun bottoms, leaving a ½-in. shell (save removed bread for another use). In a large skillet, heat butter over medium heat. Add the shrimp; cook and stir 3-4 minutes or until shrimp turn pink.
2. In a small bowl, mix mayonnaise, lemon juice, dill, salt and pepper until blended. Add shrimp; toss to coat.

Spoon shrimp mixture into the bun bottoms. If desired, top with lettuce and tomato. Replace tops.

FAST FIX
HALIBUT STEAKS WITH PAPAYA MINT SALSA

The combination of zesty fruit salsa and tender halibut makes this dish the catch of the day!
—**SONYA LABBE** WEST HOLLYWOOD, CA

START TO FINISH: 20 MIN.
MAKES: 4 SERVINGS

- 1 medium papaya, peeled, seeded and chopped
- ¼ cup chopped red onion
- ¼ cup fresh mint leaves
- 1 teaspoon finely chopped chipotle pepper in adobo sauce
- 2 tablespoons olive oil, divided
- 1 tablespoon honey
- 4 halibut steaks (6 ounces each)

1. In a small bowl, combine the papaya, onion, mint, chipotle pepper, 1 tablespoon oil and honey. Cover and refrigerate until serving.
2. In a large skillet, cook halibut in the remaining oil for 4-6 minutes on each side or until the fish flakes easily with a fork. Serve with salsa.

STUFFED-OLIVE COD

FAST FIX

POACHED SALMON WITH DILL & TURMERIC

This is among my husband's favorites because it's always juicy and delicious. It's a quick way to prepare salmon, and the robust turmeric doesn't overpower the taste of the fish.

—EVELYN BANKER ELMHURST, NY

START TO FINISH: 30 MIN.
MAKES: 4 SERVINGS

- 1 tablespoon canola oil
- ¼ teaspoon cumin seeds
- 1 pound Yukon Gold potatoes (about 2 medium), finely chopped
- 1¼ teaspoons salt, divided
- ⅛ teaspoon plus ¼ teaspoon ground turmeric, divided
- 2 tablespoons chopped fresh dill, divided
- 4 salmon fillets (1 inch thick and 4 ounces each)
- 8 fresh dill sprigs
- 2 teaspoons grated lemon peel
- 2 tablespoons lemon juice
- 1 cup (8 ounces) reduced-fat plain yogurt
- ¼ teaspoon pepper

1. In a large skillet, heat the oil and cumin over medium heat 1-2 minutes or until seeds are toasted, stirring occasionally. Stir in the potatoes, ½ teaspoon salt and ⅛ teaspoon turmeric. Cook, covered, on medium-low 10-12 minutes or until tender. Stir in 1 tablespoon chopped dill; cook, uncovered, 1 minute. Remove from the heat.

2. Meanwhile, place salmon, skin side down, in a large skillet with high sides. Add dill sprigs, lemon peel, lemon juice, ½ teaspoon salt, remaining turmeric and enough water to cover salmon. Bring just to a boil. Adjust heat to maintain a gentle simmer. Cook, uncovered, 7-9 minutes or until the fish just begins to flake easily with a fork.

3. In a small bowl, mix yogurt, pepper and the remaining 1 tablespoon chopped dill and ¼ teaspoon salt. Serve with salmon and potatoes.

FAST FIX

STUFFED-OLIVE COD

Take advantage of the olive bar in your supermarket to put a new twist on cod. This lighter entree is a weeknight lifesaver.

—TRIA OLSEN QUEEN CREEK, AZ

START TO FINISH: 25 MIN.
MAKES: 4 SERVINGS

- 4 cod fillets (6 ounces each)
- 1 teaspoon dried oregano
- ¼ teaspoon salt
- 1 medium lemon, thinly sliced
- 1 shallot, thinly sliced
- ⅓ cup garlic-stuffed olives, halved
- 2 tablespoons water
- 2 tablespoons olive juice

1. Place fillets in a large nonstick skillet coated with cooking spray. Sprinkle with oregano and salt; top with lemon and shallot.

2. Scatter olives around fish; add the water and olive juice. Bring to a boil. Reduce heat to low; gently cook, covered, 8-10 minutes or until fish just begins to flake easily with a fork.

---

(5) INGREDIENTS FAST FIX

SPICY GARLIC SHRIMP

Zesty, spicy and simple, these garlicky shrimp are perfect for a party. For more fire, substitute minced fresh hot chili peppers for the red pepper flakes.

—JASMIN BARON LIVONIA, NY

START TO FINISH: 25 MIN.
MAKES: ABOUT 2½ DOZEN

- 1 pound uncooked medium shrimp
- 3 garlic cloves, minced
- ½ teaspoon crushed red pepper flakes
- 3 tablespoons butter
- ½ cup white wine

1. Peel and devein the shrimp, leaving the tails on.

2. In a large skillet over medium heat, cook garlic and pepper flakes in butter for 1 minute. Add shrimp; cook and stir until shrimp turn pink. Remove from the pan and set aside. Add wine to the pan; cook until liquid is reduced by half. Return the shrimp to skillet; heat through.

FETA SHRIMP SKILLET

On our honeymoon in Greece, my husband and I had a dish like this one, so I tried to re-create the flavors in this recipe when we got home. When I make it now, it brings back such wonderful memories.

—**SONALI RUDER** NEW YORK, NY

START TO FINISH: 30 MIN.
MAKES: 4 SERVINGS

- 1 tablespoon olive oil
- 1 medium onion, finely chopped
- 3 garlic cloves, minced
- 1 teaspoon dried oregano
- ½ teaspoon pepper
- ¼ teaspoon salt
- 2 cans (14½ ounces each) diced tomatoes, undrained
- ¼ cup white wine, optional
- 1 pound uncooked medium shrimp, peeled and deveined
- 2 tablespoons minced fresh parsley
- ¾ cup crumbled feta cheese

1. In a large nonstick skillet, heat oil over medium-high heat. Add onion; cook and stir 4-6 minutes or until tender. Add the garlic and seasonings; cook 1 minute longer. Stir in tomatoes and, if desired, wine. Bring to a boil. Reduce heat; simmer, uncovered, 5-7 minutes or until the sauce is slightly thickened.

2. Add the shrimp and parsley; cook 5-6 minutes or until shrimp turn pink, stirring occasionally. Remove from heat; sprinkle with cheese. Let stand, covered, until cheese is softened.

FETA SHRIMP SKILLET

**COD WITH BACON &
BALSAMIC TOMATOES**

**CREAMY SALMON
LINGUINE**

(5)INGREDIENTS **FAST FIX** ▶

COD WITH BACON & BALSAMIC TOMATOES

Let's face it, everything really is better with bacon. I fry it up, add cod fillets to the pan and finish with a big, tomato pop.

—MAUREEN MCCLANAHAN ST. LOUIS, MO

START TO FINISH: 30 MIN.
MAKES: 4 SERVINGS

- 4 center-cut bacon strips, chopped
- 4 cod fillets (5 ounces each)
- ½ teaspoon salt
- ¼ teaspoon pepper
- 2 cups grape tomatoes, halved
- 2 tablespoons balsamic vinegar

1. In a large skillet, cook the bacon over medium heat until crisp, stirring occasionally. Remove with a slotted spoon; drain on paper towels.
2. Sprinkle the fillets with salt and pepper. Add fillets to the bacon drippings; cook over medium-high heat 4-6 minutes on each side or until fish just begins to flake easily with a fork. Remove and keep warm.
3. Add tomatoes to skillet; cook and stir 2-4 minutes or until tomatoes are softened. Stir in vinegar; reduce heat to medium-low. Cook 1-2 minutes longer or until the sauce is thickened. Serve cod with the tomato mixture and bacon.

FAST FIX ▶

CREAMY SALMON LINGUINE

Salmon gives this creamy pasta toss a luxurious taste and texture. We love it as is, but you could easily sub in any veggies you have on hand for the broccoli.

—JACOB KITZMAN SEATTLE, WA

START TO FINISH: 25 MIN.
MAKES: 5 SERVINGS

- 8 ounces uncooked linguine
- 1 bunch broccoli, cut into florets
- 2 tablespoons butter
- 2 garlic cloves, minced
- 2 cups heavy whipping cream
- 2 tablespoons lemon juice
- 1 pound fully cooked salmon, flaked
- ¼ teaspoon salt
- ¼ teaspoon pepper
- 1 cup shredded Parmesan cheese
- 3 tablespoons minced fresh basil or
  1 tablespoon dried basil
- 2 tablespoons capers, drained
- 2 teaspoons grated lemon peel

1. Cook the linguine according to the package directions, adding broccoli during the last 5 minutes of cooking.
2. Meanwhile, in a large skillet, heat the butter over medium heat. Add garlic; cook and stir 1 minute. Stir in the cream and lemon juice. Bring to a boil. Reduce the heat; simmer, uncovered, 2-3 minutes or until slightly thickened, stirring constantly.
3. Add salmon, salt and pepper; heat through. Drain linguine and broccoli; add to skillet. Stir in the cheese, basil, capers and lemon peel.

SHRIMP ORZO WITH FETA

My Nana cooked wonderful *Taste of Home* recipes. As I got older, she let me help her. We really cherish this shrimp and orzo recipe.
—**SARAH HUMMEL** MOON TOWNSHIP, PA

START TO FINISH: 25 MIN.
MAKES: 4 SERVINGS

- 1¼ cups uncooked whole wheat orzo pasta
- 2 tablespoons olive oil
- 2 garlic cloves, minced
- 2 medium tomatoes, chopped
- 2 tablespoons lemon juice
- 1¼ pounds uncooked shrimp (26-30 per pound), peeled and deveined
- 2 tablespoons minced fresh cilantro
- ¼ teaspoon pepper
- ½ cup crumbled feta cheese

1. Cook orzo according to package directions. Meanwhile, in a large skillet, heat the oil over medium heat. Add garlic; cook and stir for 1 minute. Add tomatoes and lemon juice. Bring to a boil. Stir in shrimp. Reduce heat; simmer, uncovered, 4-5 minutes or until shrimp turn pink.

2. Drain the orzo. Add orzo, cilantro and pepper to shrimp mixture; heat through. Sprinkle with feta cheese.

FAST FIX
SCALLOPS WITH CHIPOTLE-ORANGE SAUCE

Tender scallops with a sprinkle of paprika and ground chipotle make this recipe a tasty way to warm up dinnertime.
—**JAN JUSTICE** CATLETTSBURG, KY

START TO FINISH: 15 MIN.
MAKES: 2 SERVINGS

- ¾ pound sea scallops
- ¼ teaspoon paprika
- ¼ teaspoon salt, divided
- 2 teaspoons butter
- ¼ cup orange juice
- ¼ teaspoon ground chipotle pepper
  Hot cooked linguine, optional
- 2 tablespoons thinly sliced green onion

1. Sprinkle scallops with paprika and ⅛ teaspoon salt. In a nonstick skillet coated with cooking spray, melt butter over medium heat. Add scallops; cook for 3-4 minutes on each side or until firm and opaque.

2. Add orange juice and remaining salt to the pan; bring to a boil. Remove from the heat; stir in chipotle pepper.
3. Serve over linguine if desired. Garnish with green onion.

⑤ INGREDIENTS FAST FIX
BACON-WRAPPED SCALLOPS WITH PINEAPPLE QUINOA

This is the first recipe I developed using quinoa as an ingredient. My husband thoroughly enjoyed helping me test it. And we both love that it can be easily prepared in under 30 minutes.
—**LAURA GREENBERG** LAKE BALBOA, CA

START TO FINISH: 30 MIN.
MAKES: 4 SERVINGS

- 1 can (14½ ounces) vegetable broth
- 1 cup quinoa, rinsed
- ¼ teaspoon salt
- ⅛ teaspoon plus ¼ teaspoon pepper, divided
- 10 bacon strips
- 16 sea scallops (about 2 pounds), side muscles removed
- 1 cup drained canned pineapple tidbits

1. In a small saucepan, bring the broth to a boil. Add quinoa, salt and ⅛ teaspoon pepper. Reduce heat; simmer, covered, 12-15 minutes or until liquid is absorbed.
2. Meanwhile, place bacon in a large nonstick skillet. Cook over medium heat, removing eight of the strips when partially cooked but not crisp. Continue cooking remaining strips until crisp. Remove to paper towels to drain. Finely chop the crisp bacon strips. Cut remaining bacon strips lengthwise in half.
3. Wrap a halved bacon strip around each scallop; secure with a toothpick. Sprinkle with remaining pepper.
4. Wipe the pan clean, if necessary; heat over medium-high heat. Add the scallops; cook 3-4 minutes on each side or until the scallops are firm and opaque.
5. Remove quinoa from heat; fluff with a fork. Stir in pineapple and chopped bacon. Serve with scallops.
NOTE *Look for quinoa in the cereal, rice or organic food aisle.*

SHRIMP ORZO WITH FETA

**PAN-ROASTED
SALMON WITH
CHERRY TOMATOES**

⑤INGREDIENTS FAST FIX

PAN-ROASTED SALMON WITH CHERRY TOMATOES

It sounds basic, but the tomato sauce here is so awesome. If you have it, use white wine instead of chicken broth. I like to serve my salmon with asparagus—just roast it alongside the fish.

—SWATI SHARAN HORSEHEADS, NY

START TO FINISH: 30 MIN.
MAKES: 4 SERVINGS

- 2 **cups cherry tomatoes, halved**
- 1 **tablespoon olive oil**
- ¼ **teaspoon kosher salt**
- ¼ **teaspoon pepper**

SALMON
- 4 **salmon fillets (6 ounces each)**
- ½ **teaspoon kosher salt**
- ¼ **teaspoon pepper**
- 1 **tablespoon olive oil**
- 2 **garlic cloves, minced**
- ¾ **cup reduced-sodium chicken broth**

1. Preheat oven to 425°. Place the tomatoes in a foil-lined 15x10x1-in. baking pan. Drizzle with oil; sprinkle with salt and pepper. Toss to coat. Roast 10-15 minutes or until tomatoes are softened, stirring occasionally.
2. Meanwhile, sprinkle fillets with salt and pepper. In a large ovenproof skillet, heat oil over medium-high heat. Add fillets; cook 3 minutes on each side. Remove from pan.
3. Add the garlic to pan; cook and stir 1 minute. Add broth, stirring to loosen browned bits from pan. Bring to a boil; cook 1-2 minutes or until the liquid is reduced by half. Stir in the roasted tomatoes; return salmon to pan. Bake 5-7 minutes or until fish just begins to flake easily with a fork.

BAJA FISH TACOS

Crisp mahi mahi will pan out beautifully when dressed up with fresh lime, cilantro and smoky adobo. One bite and you might be hooked!

—**BROOKE KELLER** LEXINGTON, KY

PREP: 30 MIN. • **COOK:** 5 MIN./BATCH
MAKES: 8 SERVINGS

- 1 cup reduced-fat ranch salad dressing
- 3 tablespoons adobo sauce
- 2 tablespoons minced fresh cilantro
- 2 tablespoons lime juice
- 2 pounds mahi mahi, cut into 1-inch strips
- ¼ teaspoon salt
- ¼ teaspoon pepper
- ⅔ cup all-purpose flour
- 3 large eggs, beaten
- 2 cups panko (Japanese) bread crumbs
- 1 cup canola oil
- 16 corn tortillas (6 inches), warmed
- 3 cups shredded cabbage
  Additional minced fresh cilantro and lime wedges

1. In a small bowl, combine the salad dressing, adobo sauce, cilantro and lime juice. Chill until serving.
2. Sprinkle mahi mahi with salt and pepper. Place the flour, eggs and bread crumbs in separate shallow bowls. Coat mahi mahi with flour, then dip in eggs and coat with bread crumbs. In a large skillet, heat the oil over medium heat; cook fish in batches for 2-3 minutes on each side or until golden brown. Drain on paper towels.
3. Place fish in tortillas; top with the cabbage, sauce mixture and additional cilantro. Serve with lime wedges.

DID YOU KNOW?

Need to thaw seafood and fish fast? Give this a try: Place fish or seafood in a leak-proof bag; submerge in cold water, changing the water every 30 minutes. Allow 1 to 2 hours per pound.

FAST FIX
SIMPLE SHRIMP PAD THAI

Stir in soy sauce and brown sugar, then add a sprinkle of cilantro and roasted peanuts, and no one will guess the secret ingredient in this dish is marinara sauce.

—**ERIN CHILCOAT** CENTRAL ISLIP, NY

START TO FINISH: 30 MIN.
MAKES: 4 SERVINGS

- 8 ounces uncooked thick rice noodles
- 1 pound uncooked medium shrimp, peeled and deveined
- 3 garlic cloves, minced
- 2 tablespoons canola oil
- 2 large eggs, beaten
- 1 cup marinara sauce
- ¼ cup reduced-sodium soy sauce
- 2 tablespoons brown sugar
- ¼ cup chopped dry roasted peanuts
  Fresh cilantro leaves
- 1 medium lime, cut into wedges
  Sriracha Asian hot chili sauce or hot pepper sauce, optional

1. Cook noodles according to package directions.
2. Meanwhile, stir-fry the shrimp and garlic in oil in a large nonstick skillet or wok until shrimp turn pink; remove and keep warm. Add eggs to skillet; cook and stir until set.
3. Add the marinara, soy sauce and brown sugar; heat through. Return shrimp to the pan. Drain the noodles; toss with shrimp mixture.
4. Sprinkle with peanuts and cilantro. Serve with the lime wedges and, if desired, Sriracha.

BASIL-LEMON
CRAB LINGUINE

FAST FIX
BASIL-LEMON CRAB LINGUINE

I always add herbs to pasta to really punch it up. This linguine looks and tastes like it's from a five-star restaurant. We love it.

—**TONYA BURKHARD** PALM COAST, FL

START TO FINISH: 25 MIN.
MAKES: 4 SERVINGS

- 1 package (9 ounces) refrigerated linguine
- ⅓ cup butter, cubed
- 1 jalapeno pepper, seeded and finely chopped
- 1 garlic clove, minced
- 1 teaspoon grated lemon peel
- 3 tablespoons lemon juice
- 2 cans (6 ounces each) lump crabmeat, drained
- ¼ cup loosely packed basil leaves, thinly sliced
- ½ teaspoon sea salt
- ¼ teaspoon freshly ground pepper

1. Cook the linguine according to package directions. Meanwhile, in a large skillet, heat butter over medium heat. Add jalapeno and garlic; cook and stir 1-2 minutes or until tender. Stir in lemon peel and juice. Add the crab; heat through, stirring gently.
2. Drain the linguine; add to skillet. Sprinkle with basil, salt and pepper; toss to combine.
NOTE *Wear disposable gloves when cutting hot peppers; the oils can burn skin. Avoid touching your face.*

PESTO FISH WITH PINE NUTS

SEARED SCALLOPS WITH CITRUS HERB SAUCE

Be sure to pat the scallops with a paper towel to remove any excess moisture. This helps create perfectly browned and tasty scallops.

—**APRIL LANE** GREENEVILLE, TN

START TO FINISH: 20 MIN.
MAKES: 2 SERVINGS

- ¾ **pound sea scallops**
- ¼ **teaspoon salt**
- ¼ **teaspoon pepper**
- ⅛ **teaspoon paprika**
- 3 **tablespoons butter, divided**
- 1 **garlic clove, minced**
- 2 **tablespoons dry sherry or chicken broth**
- 1 **tablespoon lemon juice**
- ⅛ **teaspoon minced fresh oregano**
- ⅛ **teaspoon minced fresh tarragon**

1. Pat scallops dry with paper towels; sprinkle with salt, pepper and paprika. In a large skillet, heat 2 tablespoons butter over medium-high heat. Add scallops; sear for 1-2 minutes on each side or until golden brown and firm. Remove from the skillet; keep warm.
2. Wipe skillet clean if necessary. Saute the garlic in remaining butter until tender; stir in sherry. Cook until liquid is almost evaporated; stir in the remaining ingredients. Serve with the scallops.

PESTO FISH WITH PINE NUTS

I love fish, and the Italian accents in here are my favorite. This is a flavorful way to get more healthy fish into your meal planning.

—**VALERY ANDERSON** STERLING HEIGHTS, MI

START TO FINISH: 15 MIN.
MAKES: 4 SERVINGS

- 2 **envelopes pesto sauce mix, divided**
- 4 **cod fillets (6 ounces each)**
- ¼ **cup olive oil**
- ½ **cup shredded Parmesan or Romano cheese**
- ½ **cup pine nuts, toasted**

1. Prepare one envelope pesto sauce mix according to package directions; set aside. Sprinkle the fillets with remaining pesto mix, patting to help mix adhere.
2. In a large skillet, the heat oil over medium heat. Add the fillets; cook 4-5 minutes on each side or until fish just begins to flake easily with a fork. Remove from heat. Sprinkle with the cheese and pine nuts. Serve with pesto sauce.
NOTE *To toast nuts, bake in a shallow pan in a 350° oven for 5-10 minutes or cook in a skillet over low heat until lightly browned, stirring occasionally.*

POTATO-CRUSTED SNAPPER

You'll reel in raves with this seafood supper. The crispy potato-crusted fillets are great with steamed green beans and rice pilaf.

—**ATHENA RUSSELL** GREENVILLE, SC

START TO FINISH: 30 MIN.
MAKES: 4 SERVINGS

- 2 **large eggs, beaten**
- 1½ **cups mashed potato flakes**
- 2 **teaspoons dried thyme**
- 4 **red snapper fillets (6 ounces each)**
- ½ **teaspoon salt**
- ¼ **teaspoon pepper**
- ¼ **cup olive oil**

1. Place the eggs in a shallow bowl. In another shallow bowl, combine potato flakes and thyme. Sprinkle fillets with salt and pepper. Dip in eggs and coat with potato mixture.
2. In a large skillet, cook the fillets in oil in batches over medium heat for 4-5 minutes on each side or until fish flakes easily with a fork.

DID YOU KNOW?

Unless you live along the coasts, most scallops are frozen when they arrive at your local store. If you manage to find fresh scallops but don't plan to cook them that day, freeze them and thaw the day before using them.

SOFT FISH TACOS

My husband Bill and I created these delicious fish tacos. The combination of tilapia and cabbage may seem unusual, but try them and you'll be convinced.
—**CARRIE BILLUPS** FLORENCE, OR

START TO FINISH: 25 MIN.
MAKES: 5 SERVINGS

- 4 **cups coleslaw mix**
- ½ **cup fat-free tartar sauce**
- ½ **teaspoon salt**
- ½ **teaspoon ground cumin**
- ¼ **teaspoon pepper**
- 1½ **pounds tilapia fillets**
- 2 **tablespoons olive oil**
- 1 **tablespoon lemon juice**
- 10 **corn tortillas (6 inches), warmed**
  Shredded cheddar cheese, chopped tomato and sliced avocado, optional

1. In a large bowl, toss the coleslaw mix, tartar sauce, salt, cumin and pepper; set aside. In a large nonstick skillet coated with cooking spray, cook tilapia in oil and lemon juice over medium heat for 4-5 minutes on each side or until the fish flakes easily with a fork.

2. Place tilapia on tortillas; top with coleslaw mixture. Serve with cheese, tomato and avocado if desired.

SEARED SCALLOPS WITH CITRUS HERB SAUCE

SOFT FISH TACOS

SPICY TILAPIA
RICE BOWL

EASY CRAB CAKES

FAST FIX ▶
SPICY TILAPIA RICE BOWL

I love eating well, and tilapia is a staple in my kitchen. Fresh vegetables are always good but take more prep time, so I like the frozen veggie blend here.
—**ROSALIN JOHNSON** TUPELO, MS

START TO FINISH: 30 MIN.
MAKES: 4 SERVINGS

- 4 tilapia fillets (4 ounces each)
- 1¼ teaspoons Cajun seasoning
- 3 tablespoons olive oil, divided
- 1 medium yellow summer squash, halved lengthwise and sliced
- 1 package (16 ounces) frozen pepper and onion stir-fry blend
- 1 can (14½ ounces) diced tomatoes, drained
- 1 envelope fajita seasoning mix
- 1 can (15 ounces) black beans, rinsed and drained
- ⅛ teaspoon salt
- ⅛ teaspoon pepper
- 3 cups hot cooked brown rice
  Optional toppings: cubed avocado, sour cream and salsa

1. Sprinkle the fillets with Cajun seasoning. In a large skillet, heat 2 tablespoons oil over medium heat. Add fillets; cook 4-6 minutes on each side or until fish just begins to flake easily with a fork. Remove and keep warm. Wipe pan clean.

2. In same skillet, heat remaining oil. Add squash; cook and stir 3 minutes. Add stir-fry blend and tomatoes; cook 6-8 minutes longer or until vegetables are tender. Stir in fajita seasoning mix; cook and stir 1-2 minutes longer or until slightly thickened.

3. In a small bowl, mix the beans, salt and pepper. Divide the rice among four serving bowls; layer with beans, vegetables and fillets. Serve the bowls with toppings as desired.

FAST FIX ▶
EASY CRAB CAKES

Canned crabmeat makes these delicate patties ideal for dinner when you're pressed for time. You can also form the crab mixture into four thick patties instead of eight cakes.
—**CHARLENE SPELOCK** APOLLO, PA

START TO FINISH: 25 MIN.
MAKES: 4 SERVINGS

- 1 cup seasoned bread crumbs, divided
- 2 green onions, finely chopped
- ¼ cup finely chopped sweet red pepper
- 1 large egg, lightly beaten
- ¼ cup reduced-fat mayonnaise
- 1 tablespoon lemon juice
- ½ teaspoon garlic powder
- ⅛ teaspoon cayenne pepper
- 2 cans (6 ounces each) crabmeat, drained, flaked and cartilage removed
- 1 tablespoon butter

1. In a large bowl, combine ⅓ cup bread crumbs, green onions, red pepper, egg, mayonnaise, lemon juice, garlic powder and cayenne; fold in crab.

2. Place remaining bread crumbs in a shallow bowl. Divide mixture into eight portions; shape into 2-in. balls. Gently coat in the bread crumbs and shape into a ½-in.-thick patty.

3. In a large nonstick skillet, heat the butter over medium-high heat. Add crab cakes; cook 3-4 minutes on each side or until golden brown.

SHRIMP TORTELLINI PASTA TOSS

When you boost cheese tortellini with shrimp and veggies, it becomes a fast and healthy meal.

—TASTE OF HOME TEST KITCHEN

START TO FINISH: 20 MIN.
MAKES: 4 SERVINGS

- 1 **package (9 ounces) refrigerated cheese tortellini**
- 1 **cup frozen peas**
- 3 **tablespoons olive oil, divided**
- 1 **pound uncooked shrimp (31-40 per pound), peeled and deveined**
- 2 **garlic cloves, minced**
- ¼ **teaspoon salt**
- ¼ **teaspoon dried thyme**
- ¼ **teaspoon pepper**

1. Cook tortellini according to the package directions, adding the peas during the last 5 minutes of cooking.
2. Meanwhile, in a large nonstick skillet, heat 2 tablespoons oil over medium-high heat. Add the shrimp; cook and stir 2 minutes. Add garlic; cook 1-2 minutes longer or until the shrimp turn pink.
3. Drain the tortellini mixture; add to skillet. Stir in salt, thyme, pepper and remaining oil; toss to coat.

TERIYAKI MAHI MAHI

This recipe is good with rice, vegetables or salad, and it works well with cod or halibut fillets, too. Blot the fish thoroughly with paper towels before cooking to allow a nice brown crust to form.

—MICHELLE IBARRIENTOS TORRANCE, CA

START TO FINISH: 20 MIN.
MAKES: 4 SERVINGS

- 4 **mahi mahi fillets (6 ounces each)**
- ¼ **teaspoon garlic powder**
- ¼ **teaspoon pepper**
- 1 **tablespoon canola oil**
- 1 **teaspoon minced fresh gingerroot**
- ¼ **cup reduced-sodium teriyaki sauce**

1. Sprinkle the mahi mahi with garlic powder and pepper. In a large skillet, cook mahi mahi in oil over medium-high heat for 4-5 minutes on each side or until fish flakes easily with a fork. Remove and keep warm.
2. In the same skillet, saute ginger for 30 seconds. Stir in teriyaki sauce; heat through. Serve over mahi mahi.

CORNMEAL CATFISH WITH AVOCADO SAUCE

CORNMEAL CATFISH WITH AVOCADO SAUCE

When I was growing up in California, my mother often made catfish. Now, I cook it with my own twist. When only frozen catfish fillets are available, I thaw them in the refrigerator overnight, and they work just as well as fresh.

—MARY LOU COOK WELCHES, OR

START TO FINISH: 25 MIN.
MAKES: 4 SERVINGS (¾ CUP SAUCE)

- 1 **medium ripe avocado, peeled and cubed**
- ⅓ **cup reduced-fat mayonnaise**
- ¼ **cup fresh cilantro leaves**
- 2 **tablespoons lime juice**
- ½ **teaspoon garlic salt**
- ¼ **cup cornmeal**
- 1 **teaspoon seafood seasoning**
- 4 **catfish fillets (6 ounces each)**
- 3 **tablespoons canola oil**
- 1 **medium tomato, chopped**

1. Place the first five ingredients in a food processor; process until blended.
2. In a shallow bowl, mix cornmeal and seafood seasoning. Dip catfish in cornmeal mixture to coat both sides; shake off excess.
3. In a large skillet, heat the oil over medium heat. Add catfish in batches; cook 4-5 minutes on each side or until fish flakes easily with a fork. Top with avocado sauce and chopped tomato.

SHRIMP TORTELLINI PASTA TOSS

SPICY VEGGIE PASTA BAKE,
PAGE 69

67

68

66

MEATLESS

Switch up the menu tonight—let crisp vegetables or cheesy pasta take over the stovetop. You won't regret it! **Creative, fresh and unique,** these recipes will turn even picky eaters into fans.

COCONUT-GINGER CHICKPEAS & TOMATOES

LINGUINE WITH BROCCOLI RABE & PEPPERS

FAST FIX

COCONUT-GINGER CHICKPEAS & TOMATOES

This is my go-to quick dish. When you add tomatoes, you can also toss in some chopped green peppers to make it even more colorful.

—MALA UDAYAMURTHY SAN JOSE, CA

START TO FINISH: 30 MIN.
MAKES: 6 SERVINGS

- 2 tablespoons canola oil
- 2 medium onions, chopped (about 1⅓ cups)
- 3 large tomatoes, seeded and chopped (about 2 cups)
- 1 jalapeno pepper, seeded and chopped
- 1 tablespoon minced fresh gingerroot
- 2 cans (15 ounces each) chickpeas or garbanzo beans, rinsed and drained
- ¼ cup water
- 1 teaspoon salt
- 1 cup light coconut milk
- 3 tablespoons minced fresh cilantro
- 4½ cups hot cooked brown rice
  Additional minced fresh cilantro, optional

1. In a large skillet, heat the oil over medium-high heat. Add the onions; cook and stir until crisp-tender. Add tomatoes, jalapeno and ginger; cook and stir 2-3 minutes longer or until tender.
2. Stir in chickpeas, water and salt; bring to a boil. Reduce heat; simmer, uncovered, 4-5 minutes or until liquid is almost evaporated. Remove from heat; stir in coconut milk and cilantro.
3. Serve with the rice; sprinkle with additional cilantro if desired.
NOTE *Wear disposable gloves when cutting hot peppers; the oils can burn skin. Avoid touching your face.*

FAST FIX

LINGUINE WITH BROCCOLI RABE & PEPPERS

Broccoli rabe is one of my favorite vegetables. Because it cooks right with the pasta, you can do two things at once. Before you know it, you've whipped up a colorful and nutritious dinner.

—GILDA LESTER MILLSBORO, DE

START TO FINISH: 25 MIN.
MAKES: 6 SERVINGS

- 1 pound broccoli rabe
- 1 package (16 ounces) linguine
- 3 tablespoons olive oil
- 2 anchovy fillets, finely chopped, optional
- 3 garlic cloves, minced
- ½ cup sliced roasted sweet red peppers
- ½ cup pitted Greek olives, halved
- ½ teaspoon crushed red pepper flakes
- ¼ teaspoon pepper
- ⅛ teaspoon salt
- ½ cup grated Romano cheese

1. Cut ½ in. off ends of broccoli rabe; trim woody stems. Cut the stems and leaves into 2-in. pieces. Cook linguine according to the package directions, adding broccoli rabe during the last 5 minutes of cooking. Drain, reserving ½ cup pasta water.
2. Meanwhile, in a large skillet, heat oil over medium-high heat. Add the anchovies and garlic; cook and stir 1 minute. Stir in red peppers, olives, pepper flakes, pepper and salt.
3. Add linguine and broccoli rabe to skillet; toss to combine, adding reserved pasta water as desired to moisten. Serve with cheese.

MOO SHU MUSHROOM WRAPS

With so many awesome veggies to choose from, I'm always playing around with the ingredients in these wraps. Sometimes I add extra protein, too: chicken, shrimp, pork, beef or tofu all work. Check for Sriracha and hoisin sauces in the international foods section of your grocery store.

—**ATHENA RUSSELL** GREENVILLE, SC

START TO FINISH: 30 MIN.
MAKES: 5 SERVINGS

- **4 teaspoons sesame or canola oil, divided**
- **4 large eggs, lightly beaten**
- **½ pound sliced fresh mushrooms**
- **1 package (12 ounces) broccoli coleslaw mix**
- **2 garlic cloves, minced**
- **2 teaspoons minced fresh gingerroot**
- **2 tablespoons rice vinegar**
- **2 tablespoons reduced-sodium soy sauce**
- **2 teaspoons Sriracha Asian hot chili sauce**
- **1 cup fresh bean sprouts**
- **½ cup hoisin sauce**
- **10 flour tortillas (6 inches), warmed**
- **6 green onions, sliced**

1. In a large nonstick skillet, heat 1 teaspoon oil over medium heat. Pour in eggs; cook and stir until the eggs are thickened and no liquid egg remains. Remove from pan.
2. In same skillet, heat the remaining oil over medium-high heat. Add the mushrooms; cook and stir until tender. Add coleslaw mix, garlic and ginger; cook 1-2 minutes longer or until slaw is crisp-tender. In a small bowl, mix vinegar, soy sauce and chili sauce; add to pan. Stir in sprouts and eggs; heat through.
3. Spread about 2 teaspoons of the hoisin sauce over each tortilla to within ¼ in. of edges. Layer with ½ cup vegetable mixture and about 1 tablespoon green onion. Roll up wraps tightly.

MOO SHU MUSHROOM WRAPS

SWEET POTATOES WITH CILANTRO BLACK BEANS

As a vegan, I'm always looking for impressive dishes to share. Sweet potatoes loaded with beans and a touch of peanut butter are one of my mom's best-loved recipes.

—**KAYLA CAPPER** OJAI, CA

START TO FINISH: 20 MIN.
MAKES: 4 SERVINGS

- **4 medium sweet potatoes (about 8 ounces each)**
- **1 tablespoon olive oil**
- **1 small sweet red pepper, chopped**
- **2 green onions, chopped**
- **1 can (15 ounces) black beans, rinsed and drained**
- **½ cup salsa**
- **¼ cup frozen corn**
- **2 tablespoons lime juice**
- **1 tablespoon creamy peanut butter**
- **1 teaspoon ground cumin**
- **¼ teaspoon garlic salt**
- **¼ cup minced fresh cilantro**
  Additional minced fresh cilantro, optional

1. Scrub the sweet potatoes; pierce several times with a fork. Place on a microwave-safe plate. Microwave, uncovered, on high 6-8 minutes or until tender, turning once.
2. Meanwhile, in a large skillet, heat the oil over medium-high heat. Add pepper and green onions; cook and stir 3-4 minutes or until tender. Stir in the beans, salsa, corn, lime juice, peanut butter, cumin and garlic salt; heat through. Stir in cilantro.
3. With a sharp knife, cut an "X" in each sweet potato. Fluff pulp with a fork. Spoon the bean mixture over potatoes. If desired, sprinkle with additional cilantro.

MEATLESS

FAST FIX

BLACK BEAN PASTA

This was something I created when I was a teenager. Now my daughter is a vegetarian, and she asks for this dinner several times a week.
—ASHLYNN AZAR BEAVERTON, OR

START TO FINISH: 25 MIN.
MAKES: 6 SERVINGS

- 9 ounces uncooked whole wheat fettuccine
- 1 tablespoon olive oil
- 1¾ cups sliced baby portobello mushrooms
- 1 garlic clove, minced
- 1 can (15 ounces) black beans, rinsed and drained
- 1 can (14½ ounces) diced tomatoes, undrained
- 1 teaspoon dried rosemary, crushed
- ½ teaspoon dried oregano
- 2 cups fresh baby spinach

1. Cook the fettuccine according to package directions. Meanwhile, in a large skillet, heat oil over medium-high heat. Add mushrooms; cook and stir 4-6 minutes or until tender. Add garlic; cook 1 minute longer.
2. Stir in the black beans, tomatoes, rosemary and oregano; heat through. Stir in spinach until wilted. Drain fettuccine; add to bean mixture and toss to combine.

FREEZE IT   FAST FIX

LEMONY CHICKPEAS

These saucy chickpeas add just a little heat to meatless Mondays. They're especially good over hot brown rice.
—APRIL STREVELL RED BANK, NJ

START TO FINISH: 30 MIN.
MAKES: 4 SERVINGS

- 2 cups uncooked instant brown rice
- 1 tablespoon olive oil
- 1 medium onion, chopped
- 2 cans (15 ounces each) chickpeas or garbanzo beans, rinsed and drained
- 1 can (14 ounces) diced tomatoes, undrained
- 1 cup vegetable broth
- ¼ teaspoon crushed red pepper flakes
- ¼ teaspoon pepper
- ½ teaspoon grated lemon peel
- 3 tablespoons lemon juice

1. Cook rice according to package directions. Meanwhile, in a large skillet, heat oil over medium heat. Add onion; cook and stir 3-4 minutes or until tender.
2. Stir in chickpeas, tomatoes, broth, pepper flakes and pepper; bring to a boil. Reduce heat; simmer, covered, 10 minutes to allow flavors to blend. Uncover; simmer 4-5 minutes or until the liquid is slightly reduced, stirring occasionally. Stir in lemon peel and lemon juice. Serve with rice.
FREEZE OPTION *Freeze cooled chickpea mixture in freezer containers. To use, partially thaw in refrigerator overnight. Heat through in a saucepan, stirring occasionally and adding a little broth if necessary.*

FAST FIX

ZIPPY ZUCCHINI PASTA

A bright mix of zucchini and canned tomatoes is delicious over quick-cooking angel hair pasta. We like the extra zip from crushed red pepper flakes.
—KATHLEEN TIMBERLAKE
DEARBORN HEIGHTS, MI

START TO FINISH: 15 MIN.
MAKES: 3 SERVINGS

- 1 package (7 ounces) angel hair pasta or thin spaghetti
- 2 small zucchini, cut into ¼-inch pieces
- 2 garlic cloves, minced
- 3 tablespoons olive oil
- 1 can (14½ ounces) Mexican diced tomatoes, undrained
- ¼ cup minced fresh parsley
- 1 teaspoon dried oregano
- ⅛ to ½ teaspoon crushed red pepper flakes

1. Cook pasta according to package directions. Meanwhile, in a large skillet, saute zucchini and garlic in oil until zucchini is crisp-tender.
2. Add the tomatoes, parsley, oregano and pepper flakes; heat through. Drain the pasta; serve with zucchini mixture.

FAST FIX

LINGUINE WITH ARTICHOKE-TOMATO SAUCE

Haven't got a clue what to make for dinner? Grab a box of pasta, a can of tomatoes and a jar of artichoke hearts, and you're well on your way to a tasty 30-minute dinner.
—MARY ANN LEE CLIFTON PARK, NY

START TO FINISH: 30 MIN.
MAKES: 6 SERVINGS

- 12 ounces uncooked linguine
- 1 can (28 ounces) whole tomatoes with basil
- 1 jar (7½ ounces) marinated quartered artichoke hearts
- 1 cup chopped sweet onion
- 2 garlic cloves, minced
- 3 tablespoons olive oil, divided
- ¼ cup capers
- ¼ cup tomato paste
- 8 fresh basil leaves, torn
- 2 teaspoons sugar
- ½ teaspoon salt
- ¼ teaspoon pepper
  Grated Parmesan cheese

1. Cook the linguine according to package directions.
2. Meanwhile, coarsely chop the tomatoes, reserving liquid. Drain the artichokes, reserving ¼ cup marinade. In a large skillet, saute onion and garlic in 2 tablespoons oil until tender. Add the tomatoes, artichokes, capers, tomato paste, basil, sugar, salt, pepper, reserved tomato liquid and the artichoke marinade.
3. Bring to a boil. Reduce heat; simmer, uncovered, for 10 minutes or until slightly thickened. Drain linguine and transfer to a large bowl. Toss with the tomato mixture and remaining oil. Sprinkle with cheese.

66 TASTEOFHOME.COM

HOMEY MAC & CHEESE

I also call this "My Grandson's Mac & Cheese." Zachary has been to Iraq and Afghanistan with both the Marines and the Navy, and I've been privileged to make his favorite casserole for him for more than 20 years.
—**ALICE BEARDSELL** OSPREY, FL

PREP: 20 MIN. • **BAKE:** 25 MIN.
MAKES: 8 SERVINGS

- 2½ **cups uncooked elbow macaroni**
- ¼ **cup butter, cubed**
- ¼ **cup all-purpose flour**
- ½ **teaspoon salt**
- ¼ **teaspoon pepper**
- 3 **cups 2% milk**
- 5 **cups (20 ounces) shredded sharp cheddar cheese, divided**
- 2 **tablespoons Worcestershire sauce**
- ½ **teaspoon paprika**

1. Preheat oven to 350°. Cook the macaroni according to the package directions for al dente.

2. Meanwhile, in a large saucepan, heat butter over medium heat. Stir in flour, salt and pepper until smooth; gradually whisk in milk. Bring to a boil, stirring constantly; cook and stir 2-3 minutes or until thickened.

3. Reduce heat. Stir in 3 cups cheese and Worcestershire sauce until the cheese is melted.

4. Drain macaroni; stir into sauce. Transfer mixture to a greased 10-in. ovenproof skillet. Bake, uncovered, 20 minutes. Top with remaining cheese; sprinkle with paprika. Bake 5-10 minutes longer or until bubbly and cheese is melted.

HOMEY MAC & CHEESE

VEGGIE BEAN TACOS

In the summer when fresh corn and just-picked tomatoes are in season, authentic Mexican dishes such as this leave you wanting that next bite. My personal preference is to serve them with a slice of lime to squeeze over the avocado.

—TONYA BURKHARD DAVIS, IL

PREP: 20 MIN. • **COOK:** 20 MIN.
MAKES: 6 SERVINGS

- 2 **cups fresh corn**
- 2 **tablespoons canola oil, divided**
- 4 **medium tomatoes, seeded and chopped**
- 3 **small zucchini, chopped**
- 1 **large red onion, chopped**
- 3 **garlic cloves, minced**
- 1 **cup black beans, rinsed and drained**
- 1 **teaspoon minced fresh oregano or ¼ teaspoon dried oregano**
- ½ **teaspoon salt**
- ¼ **teaspoon pepper**
- 12 **corn tortillas (6 inches), warmed**
- ¾ **cup shredded Monterey Jack cheese**
- ¼ **cup salsa verde**
- 1 **medium ripe avocado, peeled and thinly sliced**
  Reduced-fat sour cream, optional

1. In a large skillet, saute the corn in 1 tablespoon oil until lightly browned. Remove and keep warm. In the same skillet, saute tomatoes, zucchini and onion in remaining oil until tender. Add garlic; cook 1 minute longer. Stir in the beans, oregano, salt, pepper and corn; heat through.

2. Divide filling among the tortillas. Top with cheese, salsa, avocado and, if desired, sour cream.

GARBANZO-VEGETABLE
GREEN CURRY

FAST FIX

GARBANZO-VEGETABLE GREEN CURRY

My son loves anything with coconut milk, so I always keep some on hand for weeknight meals like this one. For a milder version, you can use the red or yellow curry paste instead of green.

—MARIE PARKER MILWAUKEE, WI

START TO FINISH: 20 MIN.
MAKES: 6 SERVINGS

- 3 **cups frozen cauliflower**
- 2 **cans (15 ounces each) garbanzo beans or chickpeas, rinsed and drained**
- 1 **can (13.66 ounces) coconut milk**
- ¼ **cup green curry paste**
- ½ **teaspoon salt**
- 2 **teaspoons cornstarch**
- 1 **tablespoon cold water**
- 1½ **cups frozen peas**
- 2 **packages (8.8 ounces each) ready-to-serve long grain rice**
- ½ **cup lightly salted cashews**

1. In a large skillet, combine the cauliflower, beans, coconut milk, curry paste and salt. Bring to a boil;

cook, uncovered, 5-6 minutes or until cauliflower is tender.

2. Combine cornstarch and water until smooth; gradually stir into the skillet. Stir in peas. Bring to a boil. Cook and stir for 2 minutes or until mixture is thickened.

3. Meanwhile, prepare rice according to the package directions. Sprinkle cauliflower mixture with cashews. Serve with rice.

MAKE IT SIZZLE

This was a very quick dinner to prepare. My love for Thai food and curries means I usually have canned coconut milk and prepared curries on hand. I also keep a variety of frozen vegetables in the freezer and canned beans in my pantry. When I read the ingredients I didn't have to purchase any extra ones. My husband and I loved it for the great flavor and I also loved the convenience! It also has become a staple in our menu of no-meat meals.

—MISSPK TASTEOFHOME.COM

SPICY VEGGIE PASTA BAKE

My dad cooked with cast-iron skillets, so when I do, I remember his amazing cooking skills. I keep the tradition going with my veggie pasta.
—SONYA GOERGEN MOORHEAD, MN

START TO FINISH: 30 MIN.
MAKES: 6 SERVINGS

- 3 cups uncooked spiral pasta
- 1 medium yellow summer squash
- 1 small zucchini
- 1 medium sweet red pepper
- 1 medium green pepper
- 1 tablespoon olive oil
- 1 small red onion, halved and sliced
- 1 cup sliced fresh mushrooms
- ½ teaspoon salt
- ¼ teaspoon pepper
- ¼ teaspoon crushed red pepper flakes
- 1 jar (24 ounces) spicy marinara sauce
- 8 ounces fresh mozzarella cheese pearls
  Grated Parmesan cheese and julienned fresh basil, optional

1. Preheat oven to 375°. Cook pasta according to package directions for al dente; drain.
2. Cut squash, zucchini and peppers into ¼-in. julienne strips. In a 12-in. cast-iron skillet, heat the oil over medium-high heat. Add the onion, mushrooms and julienned vegetables; cook and stir 5-7 minutes or until crisp-tender. Stir in the seasonings. Add marinara sauce and pasta; toss to combine. Top with cheese pearls.
3. Transfer to the oven; bake, uncovered, 10-15 minutes or until cheese is melted. If desired, sprinkle with Parmesan cheese and basil before serving.

PENNE WITH TOMATOES & WHITE BEANS

PENNE WITH TOMATOES & WHITE BEANS

I learned how to make this dish from friends in Genoa, Italy, where cooks are known for creating mouthwatering combos of veggies, pasta and beans. You can sub feta cheese to give this a nice Greek twist.
—TRISHA KRUSE EAGLE, ID

START TO FINISH: 30 MIN.
MAKES: 4 SERVINGS

- 8 ounces uncooked penne pasta
- 2 tablespoons olive oil
- 1 garlic clove, minced
- 2 cans (14½ ounces each) Italian diced tomatoes, undrained
- 1 can (15 ounces) white kidney or cannellini beans, rinsed and drained
- 1 package (10 ounces) fresh spinach, trimmed
- ¼ cup sliced ripe olives
- ½ teaspoon salt
- ¼ teaspoon pepper
- ½ cup grated Parmesan cheese

1. Cook pasta according to package directions. Meanwhile, in a large skillet, heat oil over medium-high heat. Add the garlic; cook and stir 1 minute. Add tomatoes and beans. Bring to a boil. Reduce heat; simmer, uncovered, 5-7 minutes to allow flavors to blend.
2. Add the spinach, olives, salt and pepper; cook and stir over medium heat until spinach is wilted. Drain the pasta; top with tomato mixture and cheese.

SPICY VEGGIE PASTA BAKE

**BROCCOLI
WITH ASIAGO,
PAGE 78**

72

77

75

SIDE DISHES & MORE

Need a **simple side dish** to quickly round out your meal? Look no further! Cook up a dazzling veggie-filled side, sensational pasta option or even a homey bread offering. **Put your skillet to work!**

SWEET POTATO FRIES
WITH BLUE CHEESE

FAST FIX

CURRIED FRIED RICE WITH PINEAPPLE

Make your own special fried rice, Khao Pad, that's popular in Thai restaurants. It has a bit of heat, a little sweetness and some crunch, too.

—**JOANNA YUEN** SAN JOSE, CA

START TO FINISH: 30 MIN.
MAKES: 8 SERVINGS

- 4 tablespoons canola oil, divided
- 2 large eggs, beaten
- 1 small onion, finely chopped
- 2 shallots, finely chopped
- 3 garlic cloves, minced
- 4 cups cold cooked rice
- 1 can (8 ounces) unsweetened pineapple chunks, drained
- ½ cup lightly salted cashews
- ½ cup frozen peas
- ⅓ cup minced fresh cilantro
- ¼ cup raisins
- 3 tablespoons chicken broth
- 2 tablespoons fish sauce
- 1½ teaspoons curry powder
- 1 teaspoon sugar
- ¼ teaspoon crushed red pepper flakes

1. In a large skillet or wok, heat 1 tablespoon oil over medium-high heat; add eggs. As eggs set, lift edges, letting the uncooked portion flow underneath. When the eggs are completely cooked, remove to a plate and keep warm.
2. In the same pan, stir-fry onion and shallots in remaining oil until tender. Add garlic; cook 1 minute longer. Stir in the rice, pineapple, cashews, peas, cilantro, raisins, broth, fish sauce, curry, sugar and pepper flakes; heat through. Chop egg into small pieces; add to rice mixture.

⑤ INGREDIENTS FAST FIX

SWEET POTATO FRIES WITH BLUE CHEESE

As a kid, sweet potatoes were definitely not my favorite. Then I tasted fresh-cut sweet potato fries recently. Holy moly; they were good after all!

—**KATRINA KRUMM** APPLE VALLEY, MN

START TO FINISH: 25 MIN.
MAKES: 2 SERVINGS

- 1 tablespoon olive oil
- 2 medium sweet potatoes (about 1¼ pounds), peeled and cut into ½-inch-thick strips
- 1 tablespoon apricot preserves
- ¼ teaspoon salt
- 3 tablespoons crumbled blue cheese

In a large skillet, heat oil over medium heat. Add the sweet potatoes; cook 12-15 minutes or until tender and lightly browned, turning occasionally. Add the preserves, stirring to coat; sprinkle with salt. Top with cheese.

⑤ INGREDIENTS FAST FIX

MUSHROOM & PEA RICE PILAF

Anything can be in a rice pilaf, so add peas and baby portobello mushrooms for a springlike burst of color and a variety of textures.

—**STACY MULLENS** GRESHAM, OR

START TO FINISH: 25 MIN.
MAKES: 6 SERVINGS

- 1 package (6.6 ounces) rice pilaf mix with toasted almonds
- 1 tablespoon butter
- 1½ cups fresh or frozen peas
- 1 cup sliced baby portobello mushrooms

1. Prepare pilaf according to the package directions.
2. In a large skillet, heat the butter over medium heat. Add peas and mushrooms; cook and stir 6-8 minutes or until tender. Stir in rice.

SKILLET SCALLOPED POTATOES

Our garden is a big inspiration when I'm cooking. This recipe turns produce from my husband's potato patch into a side dish we want to eat at every meal.

—LORI DANIELS BEVERLY, WV

START TO FINISH: 30 MIN.
MAKES: 4 SERVINGS

- 1 tablespoon butter
- 1 pound small red potatoes, thinly sliced (about 3 cups)
- 1 tablespoon dried minced onion
- ¾ cup chicken broth
- ½ cup half-and-half cream
- ¾ teaspoon salt
- ¼ teaspoon pepper
- 1 cup (4 ounces) shredded cheddar cheese

1. In a large nonstick skillet, heat butter over medium heat. Add the potatoes and onion; cook and stir 5 minutes.

2. Stir in broth, cream, salt and pepper. Bring to a boil. Reduce heat; simmer, covered, 10-12 minutes or until potatoes are tender. Sprinkle with the cheese; cook, covered, 2-3 minutes longer or until cheese is melted.

(5) INGREDIENTS FAST FIX

LEMONY GREEN BEANS

You can throw this dish together in minutes using ingredients you probably already have on hand. It doesn't get much better than that!

—JENNIFER TARANTINO RUTHERFORD, NJ

START TO FINISH: 20 MIN.
MAKES: 6 SERVINGS

- ¼ cup chicken broth
- 2 tablespoons olive oil
- 1½ pounds fresh green beans, trimmed
- ¾ teaspoon lemon-pepper seasoning
  Lemon wedges

In a large skillet, heat chicken broth and oil over medium-high heat. Add the green beans; cook and stir until crisp-tender. Sprinkle with lemon-pepper. Serve with lemon wedges.

SKILLET SCALLOPED POTATOES

LEMONY GREEN BEANS

CREAMY SKILLET NOODLES WITH PEAS

ZUCCHINI CHEDDAR SAUTE

(5) INGREDIENTS FAST FIX

CREAMY SKILLET NOODLES WITH PEAS

I've made this creamy noodle side for years. Since both kids and adults go for it, I keep the ingredients on hand at all times.
—**ANITA GROFF** PERKIOMENVILLE, PA

START TO FINISH: 25 MIN.
MAKES: 6 SERVINGS

- ¼ cup butter, cubed
- 2 tablespoons canola oil
- 5 cups uncooked fine egg noodles
- 2½ cups frozen peas (about 10 ounces)
- 2½ cups chicken broth
- 1 cup half-and-half cream
- ½ teaspoon salt
- ¼ teaspoon pepper

In a large skillet, heat butter and oil over medium heat. Add noodles; cook and stir 2-3 minutes or until lightly browned. Stir in peas, broth, cream, salt and pepper. Bring to a boil. Reduce heat; simmer, covered, 10-12 minutes or until noodles are tender, stirring occasionally.

FAST FIX

ZUCCHINI CHEDDAR SAUTE

When zucchini in your garden ripens all at once, try my saute method and sprinkle with cheese and toppings. We sometimes add other quick-cooking veggies.
—**MARGARET DRYE** PLAINFIELD, NH

START TO FINISH: 25 MIN.
MAKES: 4 SERVINGS

- 3 tablespoons butter
- ¾ cup chopped onion
- 1½ teaspoons dried basil
- 4 cups coarsely shredded zucchini
- 1 large garlic clove, minced
- ¾ teaspoon salt
- ¼ teaspoon pepper
- 1 cup (4 ounces) shredded cheddar cheese
- 2 medium tomatoes, cut into ¾-inch pieces
- 3 tablespoons sliced ripe olives

1. In a large skillet, heat the butter over medium heat. Add the onion and basil; cook and stir 4-5 minutes or until onion is tender. Add the zucchini and garlic; cook and stir over medium-high heat 2-3 minutes or just until the zucchini is tender. Stir in salt and pepper.

2. Top with cheese, tomatoes and olives. Cook, covered, on low about 1 minute or until cheese is melted.

DID YOU KNOW?

To properly saute vegetables, you'll need a small amount of oil or butter and a skillet or saute pan. Cook the vegetables quickly, only for the time called for in a recipe. Also, don't forget to stir frequently!

BRANDY-GLAZED CARROTS

I found this recipe about 10 years ago in an old cookbook. I changed the sugar it called for to honey. Once the carrots are glazed, they are not just delicious, but they look pretty, too.

—**TAMMY LANDRY** SAUCIER, MS

START TO FINISH: 30 MIN.
MAKES: 12 SERVINGS (¾ CUP EACH)

- 3 **pounds fresh baby carrots**
- ½ **cup butter, cubed**
- ½ **cup honey**
- ¼ **cup brandy**
- ¼ **cup minced fresh parsley**
- ½ **teaspoon salt**
- ¼ **teaspoon pepper**

In a large skillet, bring ½ in. of water to a boil. Add carrots. Cover and cook for 5-9 minutes or until crisp-tender. Drain and set aside. In the same skillet, cook butter and honey over medium heat until butter is melted. Remove from heat; stir in brandy. Bring to a boil; cook until the liquid is reduced to about ½ cup. Add the carrots, parsley, salt and pepper; heat through.

HOMEMADE TORTILLAS

I usually have to double this recipe because we go through tortillas so quickly. Soft, chewy and simple, the homemade ones will win your family over from the packaged kind!

—**KRISTIN VAN DYKEN** KENNEWICK, WA

START TO FINISH: 30 MIN.
MAKES: 8 TORTILLAS

- 2 **cups all-purpose flour**
- ½ **teaspoon salt**
- ¾ **cup water**
- 3 **tablespoons olive oil**

1. In a large bowl, combine flour and salt. Stir in water and oil. Turn onto a floured surface; knead 10-12 times, adding a little flour or water if needed to achieve a smooth dough. Let rest for 10 minutes.
2. Divide dough into eight portions. On a lightly floured surface, roll each portion into a 7-in. circle.
3. In a large nonstick skillet coated with cooking spray, cook the tortillas over medium heat for 1 minute on each side or until lightly browned. Keep warm.

CRANBERRY-WALNUT
BRUSSELS SPROUTS

CRANBERRY-WALNUT BRUSSELS SPROUTS

Brussels sprouts are a food that finicky eaters often refuse to eat, but this recipe may change their minds. You can also add garlic and dried fruits for extra flavor.

—**JENNIFER ARMELLINO** LAKE OSWEGO, OR

START TO FINISH: 20 MIN.
MAKES: 4 SERVINGS

- ¼ **cup olive oil**
- 1 **pound fresh Brussels sprouts, trimmed and halved lengthwise**
- ½ **cup dried cranberries**
- 2 **tablespoons water**
- ⅓ **cup chopped walnuts**
- 2 **tablespoons balsamic vinegar**

1. In a large skillet, heat oil over medium heat. Place the Brussels sprouts in pan, cut side down; cook 4-5 minutes or until the Brussels sprout bottoms are browned.
2. Add cranberries and water; cook, covered, 1-2 minutes or until Brussels sprouts are crisp-tender. Stir in the walnuts; cook and stir until water is evaporated. Stir in vinegar.

BRANDY-GLAZED
CARROTS

FAST FIX

LOADED CHEDDAR-CORN POTATO PATTIES

Golden, crunchy and delicious mashed potato patties are brimming with cheese, corn and green onions. These crispy little loaded potato patties are a perfect side dish, but they can do double-duty: if you make them smaller, they become a hand-held appetizer.

—**DARLENE BRENDEN** SALEM, OR

START TO FINISH: 30 MIN.
MAKES: 1 DOZEN (1 CUP SAUCE)

- 1 cup (8 ounces) sour cream
- 2 tablespoons plus ⅓ cup thinly sliced green onions
- 2 cups mashed potato flakes
- ⅓ cup cornmeal
- 1¾ teaspoons garlic salt
- ½ teaspoon smoked paprika
- 2 cups 2% milk
- 1 package (10 ounces) frozen corn, thawed
- 1 cup (4 ounces) shredded extra-sharp cheddar cheese

1. In a small bowl, mix sour cream and 2 tablespoons of the green onion; refrigerate until serving.

2. In a large bowl, mix the potato flakes, cornmeal, garlic salt and paprika. Add the milk, corn, cheese and remaining green onions; mix until blended. Using ½ cupfuls, shape mixture into twelve 3½-in. patties.

3. Heat a large nonstick skillet coated with cooking spray over medium heat. Cook the patties in batches for 2-3 minutes on each side or until golden brown. Serve with the sauce.

LOADED CHEDDAR-CORN POTATO PATTIES

RIGATONI
CHARD TOSS

3 tablespoons butter, softened
2 teaspoons salt
½ cup sugar
1 cup mashed cooked butternut
squash
5 to 5½ cups all-purpose flour,
divided

1. In a large bowl, dissolve yeast in milk and water. Add the butter, salt, sugar, squash and 3 cups flour; beat until smooth. Add enough remaining flour to form a soft dough.
2. Turn onto a floured surface; knead dough until smooth and elastic, about 6-8 minutes. Place in a greased bowl, turning once to grease top. Cover and let rise in a warm place until doubled, about 1 hour.
3. Punch the dough down. Form into rolls; place rolls in two greased 10-in. cast-iron skillets or 9-in. round baking pans. Cover and let rise until doubled, about 30 minutes.
4. Bake at 375° for 20-25 minutes or until golden brown.

RIGATONI CHARD TOSS

I try to get my firefighter husband to eat more fruits and veggies. Fresh chard and tomatoes add fiber and vitamins, but we especially love this recipe for the taste.
—**CAROLYN KUMPE** EL DORADO, CA

PREP: 25 MIN. • **COOK:** 20 MIN.
MAKES: 11 SERVINGS

8 ounces uncooked rigatoni or large
tube pasta
2 tablespoons olive oil
1 bunch Swiss chard, coarsely
chopped
1 small onion, thinly sliced
2 garlic cloves, minced
3 medium tomatoes, chopped
1 can (15 ounces) white kidney or
cannellini beans, rinsed and
drained
½ teaspoon salt
⅛ teaspoon crushed red pepper
flakes
⅛ teaspoon fennel seed, crushed
⅛ teaspoon pepper
¼ cup minced fresh basil
½ cup grated Parmesan cheese

1. Cook the rigatoni according to package directions.
2. Meanwhile, in a large skillet, heat oil over medium-high heat. Add the Swiss chard and onion; cook and stir 4 minutes. Add garlic; cook 2 minutes longer. Stir in the tomatoes, beans, salt, pepper flakes, fennel and pepper. Cook 3-4 minutes longer or until the chard is tender.
3. Drain rigatoni, reserving ¼ cup pasta water. Add rigatoni, pasta water and basil to skillet; toss to combine. Serve with cheese.

BUTTERNUT SQUASH ROLLS

With their cheery yellow color and tantalizing aroma, these warm rolls will brighten your buffet table. I've found that bread is a surprising way to take advantage of squash from the garden.
—**BERNICE MORRIS** MARSHFIELD, MO

PREP: 30 MIN. + RISING • **BAKE:** 20 MIN.
MAKES: 2 DOZEN

1 package (¼ ounce) active dry
yeast
1 cup warm milk (110° to 115°)
¼ cup warm water (110° to 115°)

(5) INGREDIENTS FAST FIX

CREAMED SPINACH & PEARL ONIONS

Even though I don't usually like spinach, this creamy dish wowed me when I was a culinary student. It's a keeper side!
—**CHELSEA PUCHEL** PICKENS, SC

START TO FINISH: 25 MIN.
MAKES: 8 SERVINGS

¼ cup butter, cubed
1 package (14.4 ounces) frozen
pearl onions, thawed and drained
2 cups heavy whipping cream
½ cup grated Parmesan cheese
½ teaspoon salt
¼ teaspoon pepper
10 ounces fresh baby spinach (about
13 cups)

1. In a large skillet, heat the butter over medium heat. Add pearl onions; cook and stir 6-8 minutes or until tender. Stir in cream. Bring to a boil; cook 6-8 minutes or until liquid is reduced by half.
2. Stir in cheese, salt and pepper. Add spinach; cook, covered, 3-5 minutes or until the spinach is wilted, stirring occasionally.

CONFETTI CORN

CONFETTI CORN

An easy corn dish is sure to dress up almost any entree. Tender corn is paired with the crunch of water chestnuts, red pepper and chopped carrot in this bright and healthy side.

—GLENDA WATTS CHARLESTON, IL

START TO FINISH: 15 MIN.
MAKES: 4 SERVINGS

- ¼ cup chopped carrot
- 1 tablespoon olive oil
- 2¾ cups fresh or frozen corn, thawed
- ¼ cup chopped water chestnuts
- ¼ cup chopped sweet red pepper

In a large skillet, saute carrot in oil until crisp-tender. Stir in the corn, water chestnuts, and red pepper; heat through.

BROCCOLI WITH ASIAGO

One of the best and simplest ways I've found to serve broccoli is with a little garlic and cheese. It's also good with Parmesan if you don't have the Asiago.

—CJINTEXAS TASTEOFHOME.COM

START TO FINISH: 20 MIN.
MAKES: 4 SERVINGS

- 1 bunch broccoli, cut into spears
- 4 teaspoons minced garlic
- 2 tablespoons olive oil
- ¼ teaspoon salt
  Dash pepper
- 1 cup (4 ounces) shaved Asiago cheese

1. Place the broccoli in a large skillet; cover with water. Bring to a boil. Reduce heat; cover and simmer for 5-7 minutes or until broccoli is tender. Drain well. Remove and keep warm.
2. In the same skillet, saute the garlic in oil for 1 minute. Stir in the broccoli, salt and pepper. Top with cheese.

BROCCOLI WITH ASIAGO

VEGGIE-TOPPED POLENTA SLICES

Even though we didn't have too many ingredients in the kitchen at the time, this amazing side came from a stroke of genius I had.

—**JENN TIDWELL** FAIR OAKS, CA

PREP: 20 MIN. • **COOK:** 20 MIN.
MAKES: 4 SERVINGS

- 1 **tube (1 pound) polenta, cut into 12 slices**
- 2 **tablespoons olive oil, divided**
- 1 **medium zucchini, chopped**
- 2 **shallots, minced**
- 2 **garlic cloves, minced**
- 3 **tablespoons reduced-sodium chicken broth**
- ½ **teaspoon pepper**
- ⅛ **teaspoon salt**
- 4 **plum tomatoes, seeded and chopped**
- 2 **tablespoons minced fresh basil or 2 teaspoons dried basil**
- 1 **tablespoon minced fresh parsley**
- ½ **cup shredded part-skim mozzarella cheese**

1. In a large nonstick skillet, cook the polenta in 1 tablespoon oil over medium heat for 9-11 minutes on each side or until golden brown.
2. Meanwhile, in another large skillet, saute zucchini in remaining oil until tender. Add the shallots and garlic; cook 1 minute longer. Add the broth, pepper and salt. Bring to a boil; cook until liquid is almost evaporated.
3. Stir in tomatoes, basil and parsley; heat through. Serve with the polenta; sprinkle with cheese.

DID YOU KNOW?

Polenta is a popular Italian dish made from cornmeal. Packaged in a tube, polenta can be found in the produce aisle, next to shredded cheese or near the refrigerated pasta.

HERBED NOODLES WITH EDAMAME

FAST FIX

HERBED NOODLES WITH EDAMAME

Here's a side dish to give your meal a pop of flavor and color. All the fresh herbs make it feel extra-special.

—**MARIE RIZZIO** INTERLOCHEN, MI

START TO FINISH: 30 MIN.
MAKES: 4 SERVINGS

- 3½ **cups uncooked egg noodles**
- 2 **tablespoons butter**
- 1 **green onion, sliced**
- 1 **tablespoon finely chopped sweet red pepper**
- ½ **cup frozen shelled edamame, thawed**
- ¼ **cup reduced-sodium chicken broth**
- 1 **tablespoon minced fresh parsley**
- 1½ **teaspoons minced fresh marjoram**
- 1½ **teaspoons minced fresh chives**
- 1 **tablespoon olive oil**
- ¼ **cup grated Romano cheese**

1. Cook noodles according to package directions. Meanwhile, in a large skillet, heat butter over medium-high heat. Add onion and red pepper; cook and stir until tender. Stir in edamame and broth; heat through. Add herbs.

2. Drain noodles and add to skillet; toss to combine. Transfer to a serving plate. Drizzle with oil and sprinkle with cheese.

---

⑤ INGREDIENTS **FAST FIX**

MINTY SUGAR SNAP PEAS

Fresh mint tastes divine on cooked sugar snap peas. It can also be a nice complement to green beans or carrots.

—**ALICE KALDAHL** RAY, ND

START TO FINISH: 10 MIN.
MAKES: 4 SERVINGS

- 3 **cups fresh sugar snap peas, trimmed**
- ¼ **teaspoon sugar**
- 2 **to 3 tablespoons minced fresh mint**
- 2 **tablespoons butter**

In a large skillet, bring 1 in. of water, peas and sugar to a boil. Reduce heat; cover and simmer for 4-5 minutes or until crisp-tender; drain. Stir in mint and butter.

SUMMER BREAKFAST
SKILLET, PAGE 91

88

89

86

BREAKFAST
& BRUNCH

Time to **wake up sleepyheads!** The promise
of omelets, sausage or pancakes will be the
rise-and-shine factor you need to get your
family moving in the morning. Waking up has
never been **so delicious!**

CREAMY EGGS
& MUSHROOMS
AU GRATIN

FRENCH BANANA PANCAKES

These pancakes are a real breakfast favorite in our family. Even our 8- and 10-year-old daughters make them all by themselves when they have friends spend the night. Now their friends' mothers often ask for the recipe.

—**CHERYL SOWERS** BAKERSFIELD, CA

PREP: 10 MIN. • **COOK:** 30 MIN.
MAKES: 5-6 SERVINGS

PANCAKES
- 1 **cup all-purpose flour**
- ¼ **cup confectioners' sugar**
- 1 **cup milk**
- 2 **large eggs**
- 3 **tablespoons butter, melted**
- 1 **teaspoon vanilla extract**
- ¼ **teaspoon salt**

FILLING
- ¼ **cup butter**
- ¼ **cup packed brown sugar**
- ¼ **teaspoon ground cinnamon**
- ¼ **teaspoon ground nutmeg**
- ¼ **cup half-and-half cream**
- 5 **to 6 firm bananas, halved lengthwise**
  Whipped cream and additional cinnamon, optional

1. Sift flour and confectioners' sugar into a bowl. Add milk, eggs, butter, vanilla and salt; beat until smooth.

2. Heat a lightly greased 6-in. skillet; add about 3 tablespoons batter, spreading to almost cover the bottom of the skillet. Cook until pancakes are lightly browned; turn and brown the other side. Remove to a wire rack. Repeat with the remaining batter (make 10-12 pancakes), greasing the skillet as needed.

3. For filling, melt butter in large skillet. Stir in brown sugar, cinnamon and nutmeg. Stir in cream and cook until slightly thickened. Add half of the bananas at a time to skillet; heat for 2-3 minutes, spooning sauce over them. Remove from the heat.

4. Roll a pancake around each banana half and place on a serving platter. Spoon sauce over pancakes. Top with whipped cream and a dash of cinnamon if desired.

CREAMY EGGS & MUSHROOMS AU GRATIN

When I want a brunch recipe that has the crowd appeal of scrambled eggs but is a little more special, I turn to this dish. The Parmesan sauce is simple but rich.

—**DEBORAH WILLIAMS** PEORIA, AZ

PREP: 15 MIN. • **COOK:** 25 MIN.
MAKES: 8 SERVINGS

- 2 **tablespoons butter**
- 1 **pound sliced fresh mushrooms**
- 1 **green onion, chopped**

SAUCE
- 2 **tablespoons butter, melted**
- 3 **tablespoons all-purpose flour**
- ½ **teaspoon salt**
- ⅛ **teaspoon pepper**
- 1 **cup 2% milk**
- ½ **cup heavy whipping cream**
- 2 **tablespoons grated Parmesan cheese**

EGGS
- 16 **large eggs**
- ¼ **teaspoon salt**
- ⅛ **teaspoon pepper**
- ¼ **cup butter, cubed**
- ½ **cup grated Parmesan cheese**
- 1 **green onion, finely chopped**

1. In a large broiler-safe skillet, heat the butter over medium-high heat. Add the mushrooms; cook and stir 4-6 minutes or until browned. Add green onion; cook 1 minute longer. Remove from the pan with a slotted spoon. Wipe skillet clean.

2. For sauce, in a small saucepan, melt butter over medium heat. Stir in flour, salt and pepper until smooth; gradually whisk in milk and cream. Bring to a boil, stirring constantly; cook and stir 2-4 minutes or until thickened. Remove from heat; stir in the cheese.

3. Preheat broiler. For eggs, in a large bowl, whisk eggs, salt and pepper until blended. In the same skillet, heat the butter over medium heat. Pour in egg mixture; cook and stir just until the eggs are thickened and no liquid egg remains. Remove from heat.

4. Spoon half of the sauce over eggs; top with mushrooms. Add remaining sauce; sprinkle with the cheese. Broil 4-5 in. from heat 4-6 minutes or until top is lightly browned. Sprinkle with green onion.

ITALIAN SAUSAGE BREAKFAST WRAPS

SAUSAGE & MUSHROOM PIZZA FRITTATA

FAST FIX ▶

ITALIAN SAUSAGE BREAKFAST WRAPS

My husband leaves for work at 4 a.m., and I want him to get a jump on the day with a hearty breakfast. I usually make half a dozen of these on Sunday and keep them in the refrigerator so he can grab one and go.

—**DAUNA HARWOOD** ELKHART, IN

START TO FINISH: 30 MIN.
MAKES: 6 SERVINGS

- ¾ pound Italian turkey sausage links, casings removed
- 1 small green pepper, finely chopped
- 1 small onion, finely chopped
- 1 medium tomato, chopped
- 4 large eggs
- 6 large egg whites
- 1 cup chopped fresh spinach
- 6 whole wheat tortillas (8 inches)
- 1 cup (4 ounces) shredded reduced-fat cheddar cheese

1. In a large skillet, cook sausage, pepper, onion and tomato over medium heat until meat is no longer pink and the vegetables are tender, breaking up sausage into crumbles; drain and return to pan.

2. In a small bowl, whisk the eggs and egg whites until blended. Add the egg mixture to the sausage. Cook and stir until eggs are thickened and no liquid egg remains. Add spinach; cook and stir just until wilted.

3. Spoon ¾ cup egg mixture across center of each tortilla; top with about 2 tablespoons cheese. Fold bottom and sides of tortilla over the filling and roll up.

FAST FIX ▶

SAUSAGE & MUSHROOM PIZZA FRITTATA

I love this frittata because the combo of fresh, bold flavors makes it stand out. It's the perfect sunny brunch item, and it takes only 30 minutes to whip up.

—**WOLFGANG HANAU** WEST PALM BEACH, FL

START TO FINISH: 30 MIN.
MAKES: 4 SERVINGS

- 4 ounces bulk Italian sausage
- 2 cups sliced fresh mushrooms
- 2 tablespoons finely chopped red onion
- 2 tablespoons finely chopped green pepper
- ¼ cup finely chopped fresh pineapple
- 6 large eggs, beaten
- 6 tablespoons marinara sauce
- 2 tablespoons shredded part-skim mozzarella cheese
- 2 tablespoons grated Parmigiano-Reggiano cheese
- 2 tablespoons minced fresh parsley

1. Preheat the broiler. In a 10-in. ovenproof skillet, cook sausage, mushrooms, onion and pepper over medium heat 6-8 minutes or until sausage is no longer pink and the vegetables are tender, breaking sausage into crumbles; drain.

2. Return sausage mixture to skillet; stir in pineapple. Pour in beaten eggs. Cook, covered, 4-6 minutes or until nearly set. Spread marinara over top; sprinkle with cheeses.

3. Broil 3-4 in. from heat 2-3 minutes or until the eggs are completely set and the cheese is melted. Let stand 5 minutes. Sprinkle with parsley; cut into wedges.

SALSA & SCRAMBLED EGG SANDWICHES

SALSA & SCRAMBLED EGG SANDWICHES

Power up with a breakfast that keeps you going all morning long. In my humble opinion, these quick sandwiches taste so much better than fast food options.

—**MARCIA CONLON** TRAVERSE CITY, MI

START TO FINISH: 25 MIN.
MAKES: 4 SERVINGS

- 8 **large eggs**
- ½ **teaspoon salt**
- ¼ **teaspoon pepper**
- 1 **cup salsa, divided**
- ½ **cup shredded cheddar cheese**
- 4 **whole wheat English muffins, split and toasted**
- ¼ **cup reduced-fat spreadable cream cheese**
- 1 **medium ripe avocado, peeled and cubed**
- ½ **small lime**
  Reduced-fat sour cream, optional

1. In a large bowl, whisk the eggs, salt and pepper. Place a large nonstick skillet coated with cooking spray over medium-high heat. Pour in the egg mixture; cook and stir until eggs are thickened and no liquid egg remains. Add ½ cup salsa and the cheese; stir gently until cheese is melted.

2. Spread cut sides of English muffins with cream cheese and remaining salsa. Top with scrambled eggs and avocado. Squeeze lime juice over tops. If desired, serve with sour cream.

MAKE IT SIZZLE

I like to add a bit of vanilla to my scrambled eggs (about a teaspoon for every 6 eggs). It's a nice, sweet change from regular scrambled eggs.

—**LARISSA M.** LONGMONT, CO

HASH BROWN &
APPLE PANCAKE

FARMERS BREAKFAST

FAST FIX
HASH BROWN &
APPLE PANCAKE

Wedges of this crispy hash make a fast and fabulous breakfast option the whole family will savor. Perked up with onions, chives and Swiss cheese, it takes only minutes to make and goes well with all kinds of brunch entrees.

—SUSAN HEIN BURLINGTON, WI

START TO FINISH: 20 MIN.
MAKES: 4 SERVINGS

- 1¼ cups frozen shredded hash brown potatoes, thawed
- ½ cup finely chopped apple
- ¼ cup finely chopped onion
- 1 large egg white
- 1 tablespoon minced fresh chives
- ¼ teaspoon salt
- ¼ teaspoon pepper
- 2 tablespoons butter, divided
- 2 tablespoons canola oil, divided
- ½ cup shredded Swiss cheese

1. In a large bowl, combine the first seven ingredients. In a large nonstick skillet, heat 1 tablespoon butter and 1 tablespoon oil over medium-high heat.
2. Spread half of the potato mixture evenly in pan; sprinkle with cheese. Top with remaining potato mixture, pressing gently into skillet. Cook 5 minutes or until bottom is browned.
3. Carefully invert pancake onto a plate. Heat remaining butter and oil in same pan. Slide pancake into skillet, browned side up. Cook for 5 minutes longer or until bottom is browned and cheese is melted. Slide pancake onto a plate; cut into four wedges.

⑤ INGREDIENTS FAST FIX
FARMERS BREAKFAST

Start off your day on a delicious note! Your family will be satisfied until lunch when you serve up this one-dish wonder.

—JEANNETTE WESTPHAL GETTYSBURG, SD

START TO FINISH: 20 MIN.
MAKES: 4-6 SERVINGS

- 6 bacon strips, diced
- 2 tablespoons diced onion
- 3 medium potatoes, cooked and cubed
- 6 large eggs, beaten
  Salt and pepper to taste
- ½ cup shredded cheddar cheese

In a skillet, cook bacon until crisp. Remove to paper towel to drain. In drippings, saute onion and potatoes until potatoes are browned, about 5 minutes. Pour eggs into skillet; cook and stir gently until eggs are set and cooked to desired doneness. Season with salt and pepper. Sprinkle with the cheese and bacon; let stand for 2-3 minutes or until cheese melts.

FAST FIX
HAM AND AVOCADO
SCRAMBLE

Hearty ham, creamy avocado and a hint of garlic—this winning egg dish has all the makings for a great breakfast, lunch or even dinner.

—ELISABETH LARSEN PLEASANT GROVE, UT

START TO FINISH: 15 MIN.
MAKES: 4 SERVINGS

- 8 large eggs
- ¼ cup 2% milk
- 1 teaspoon garlic powder
- ¼ teaspoon pepper
- 1 cup cubed fully cooked ham
- 1 tablespoon butter
- 1 medium ripe avocado, peeled and cubed
- 1 cup (4 ounces) shredded Colby-Monterey Jack cheese

In a large bowl, whisk the eggs, milk, garlic powder and pepper; stir in ham. In a large skillet, melt the butter over medium-high heat. Add egg mixture; cook and stir until almost set. Stir in avocado and cheese. Cook and stir until completely set.

FARMERS BREAKFAST

CALICO SCRAMBLED EGGS

FAST FIX

When you're scrambling to get a meal on the table, this recipe is "eggs-actly" what you need in a pinch. There's a short ingredient list, and cooking is kept to a minimum.
—TASTE OF HOME TEST KITCHEN

START TO FINISH: 20 MIN.
MAKES: 4 SERVINGS

- 8 large eggs
- ¼ cup 2% milk
- ⅛ to ¼ teaspoon dill weed
- ⅛ to ¼ teaspoon salt
- ⅛ to ¼ teaspoon pepper
- 1 tablespoon butter
- ½ cup chopped green pepper
- ¼ cup chopped onion
- ½ cup chopped fresh tomato

1. In a bowl, whisk the first five ingredients until blended. In a 12-in. nonstick skillet, heat butter over medium-high heat. Add green pepper and onion; cook and stir until tender. Remove from pan.
2. In the same pan, pour in the egg mixture; cook and stir over medium heat until eggs begin to thicken. Add the tomato and pepper mixture; cook until heated through and no liquid egg remains, stirring gently.

SWEET POTATO PANCAKES WITH CINNAMON CREAM

Topped with a decadent cinnamon cream, these pancakes are an ideal morning dish for celebrating the tastes and aromas of fall.
—TAMMY REX NEW TRIPOLI, PA

PREP: 25 MIN. • **COOK:** 5 MIN./BATCH
MAKES: 12 SERVINGS (1½ CUPS TOPPING)

- 8 ounces cream cheese, softened
- ¼ cup packed brown sugar
- ½ teaspoon ground cinnamon
- ½ cup sour cream

PANCAKES
- 6 large eggs
- ¾ cup all-purpose flour
- ½ teaspoon ground nutmeg
- ½ teaspoon salt
- ¼ teaspoon pepper
- 6 cups shredded sweet potatoes (about 3 large)
- 3 cups shredded peeled apples (about 3 large)
- ⅓ cup grated onion
- ½ cup canola oil

1. In a small bowl, beat the cream cheese, brown sugar and cinnamon until blended; beat in the sour cream. Set aside.
2. In a large bowl, whisk the eggs, flour, nutmeg, salt and pepper. Add the sweet potatoes, apples and onion; toss to coat.
3. In a large nonstick skillet, heat 2 tablespoons oil over medium heat. Working in batches, drop sweet potato mixture by ⅓ cupfuls into oil; press slightly to flatten. Fry for 2-3 minutes on each side until golden brown, using remaining oil as needed. Drain the pancakes on paper towels. Serve with cinnamon topping.

SOUTHWEST TORTILLA SCRAMBLE

⑤ INGREDIENTS FAST FIX

Here's my version of a deconstructed breakfast burrito that's actually good for you. Go for hefty corn tortillas, because sometimes flour ones don't hold up and get lost in the scramble.
—CHRISTINE SCHENHER EXETER, CA

START TO FINISH: 15 MIN.
MAKES: 2 SERVINGS

- 4 large egg whites
- 2 large eggs
- ¼ teaspoon pepper
- 2 corn tortillas (6 inches), halved and cut into strips
- ¼ cup chopped fresh spinach
- 2 tablespoons shredded reduced-fat cheddar cheese
- ¼ cup salsa

1. In a large bowl, whisk egg whites, eggs and pepper. Stir in the tortillas, spinach and cheese.
2. Heat a large skillet coated with cooking spray over medium heat. Pour in egg mixture; cook and stir until the eggs are thickened and no liquid egg remains. Top with salsa.

HAM STEAKS WITH GRUYERE, BACON & MUSHROOMS

FAST FIX

Here's a meaty breakfast with a big "wow" factor. It's one of my favorites because the Gruyere cheese, bacon and fresh mushrooms in the topping are such a savory combination.
—MARY LISA SPEER PALM BEACH, FL

START TO FINISH: 25 MIN.
MAKES: 4 SERVINGS

- 2 tablespoons butter
- ½ pound sliced fresh mushrooms
- 1 shallot, finely chopped
- 2 garlic cloves, minced
- ⅛ teaspoon coarsely ground pepper
- 1 fully cooked boneless ham steak (about 1 pound), cut into four pieces
- 1 cup (4 ounces) shredded Gruyere cheese
- 4 bacon strips, cooked and crumbled
- 1 tablespoon minced fresh parsley, optional

1. In a large nonstick skillet, heat butter over medium-high heat. Add mushrooms and shallot; cook and stir 4-6 minutes or until tender. Add the garlic and pepper; cook 1 minute longer. Remove from pan; keep warm. Wipe skillet clean.
2. In the same skillet, cook ham over medium heat for 3 minutes. Turn; sprinkle with the cheese and bacon. Cook, covered, 2-4 minutes longer or until the cheese is melted and the ham is heated through. Serve with the mushroom mixture. If desired, sprinkle with parsley.

FRESH CORN OMELET

I throw in homegrown corn and from-scratch salsa when I make this super omelet. Sprinkle onions, mushrooms, peppers and breakfast meat on top to customize the dish.

—**WILLIAM STONE** ROBSON, WV

START TO FINISH: 25 MIN.
MAKES: 4 SERVINGS

- 10 **large eggs**
- 2 **tablespoons water**
- ¼ **teaspoon salt**
- ¼ **teaspoon pepper**
- 2 **teaspoons plus 2 tablespoons butter, divided**
- 1 **cup fresh or frozen corn, thawed**
- ½ **cup shredded cheddar cheese**
  Fresh salsa

1. In a small bowl, whisk the eggs, water, salt and pepper until blended. In a large nonstick skillet, heat 2 teaspoons butter over medium heat. Add corn; cook and stir 1-2 minutes or until tender. Remove from pan.

2. In same pan, heat 1 tablespoon butter over medium-high heat. Pour in half of the egg mixture. Mixture should set immediately at edges. As eggs set, push cooked portions toward the center, letting uncooked eggs flow underneath. When eggs are thickened and no liquid egg remains, spoon half of the corn on one side; sprinkle with ¼ cup cheese. Fold omelet in half. Cut in half; slide each half onto a plate.

3. Repeat with remaining butter, egg mixture and filling. Serve with salsa.

FRESH CORN OMELET

BREAKFAST SAUSAGE PATTIES

MEDITERRANEAN BROCCOLI & CHEESE OMELET

FREEZE IT

BREAKFAST SAUSAGE PATTIES

Buttermilk is the secret ingredient that keeps these pork patties moist, while a blend of seasonings creates an absolutely wonderful taste.

—HARVEY KEENEY MANDAN, ND

PREP: 30 MIN. • **COOK:** 10 MIN./BATCH
MAKES: 20 PATTIES

- ¾ cup buttermilk
- 2¼ teaspoons kosher salt
- 1½ teaspoons rubbed sage
- 1½ teaspoons brown sugar
- 1½ teaspoons pepper
- ¾ teaspoon dried marjoram
- ¾ teaspoon dried savory
- ¾ teaspoon cayenne pepper
- ¼ teaspoon ground nutmeg
- 2½ pounds ground pork

1. In a large bowl, combine the buttermilk and seasonings. Add pork; mix lightly but thoroughly. Shape into twenty 3-in. patties.
2. In a large skillet coated with cooking spray, cook patties in batches over medium heat 5-6 minutes on each side or until a thermometer reads 160°. Remove to paper towels to drain.

FREEZE OPTION *Wrap each cooked, cooled patty in plastic wrap; transfer to a resealable plastic freezer bag. May be frozen for up to 3 months.*

TO USE FROZEN PATTIES *Unwrap patties and place on a baking sheet coated with cooking spray. Bake at 350° for 15 minutes on each side or until heated through.*

FAST FIX

MEDITERRANEAN BROCCOLI & CHEESE OMELET

My Italian mother-in-law taught me to make this omelet years ago—she would make it for breakfast, lunch or dinner and eat it on Italian bread.

—MARY LICATA PEMBROKE PINES, FL

START TO FINISH: 30 MIN.
MAKES: 4 SERVINGS

- 2½ cups fresh broccoli florets
- 6 eggs
- ¼ cup 2% milk
- ½ teaspoon salt
- ¼ teaspoon pepper
- ⅓ cup grated Romano cheese
- ⅓ cup sliced pitted Greek olives
- 1 tablespoon olive oil
  Shaved Romano cheese and minced fresh parsley

1. Preheat broiler. In a large saucepan, place the steamer basket over 1 in. of water. Place broccoli in basket. Bring water to a boil. Reduce heat to a simmer; steam, covered, 4-6 minutes or until crisp-tender.
2. In a large bowl, whisk the eggs, milk, salt and pepper. Stir in cooked broccoli, grated cheese and olives. In a 10-in. ovenproof skillet, heat oil over medium heat; pour in the egg mixture. Cook, uncovered, for 4-6 minutes or until nearly set.
3. Broil 3-4 in. from heat 2-4 minutes or until eggs are completely set. Let stand 5 minutes. Cut omelet into wedges. Sprinkle the wedges with shaved cheese and parsley.

ASPARAGUS OMELET TORTILLA WRAP

Since whole grains, veggies and protein are in this omelet, all I have to do is add a side of fresh fruit for a healthy breakfast. Instead of asparagus, sometimes I make this omelet with fresh spinach.

—**BONITA SUTER** LAWRENCE, MI

START TO FINISH: 20 MIN.
MAKES: 1 SERVING

- 1 **large egg**
- 2 **large egg whites**
- 1 **tablespoon fat-free milk**
- 2 **teaspoons grated Parmesan cheese**
- ⅛ **teaspoon pepper**
- 4 **fresh asparagus spears, trimmed and sliced**
- 1 **teaspoon butter**
- 1 **green onion, chopped**
- 1 **whole wheat tortilla (8 inches), warmed**

1. In a small bowl, whisk the first five ingredients until blended. Place a small nonstick skillet coated with cooking spray over medium heat; add asparagus. Cook and stir 3-4 minutes or until crisp-tender. Remove from the pan.
2. In the same skillet, heat butter over medium-high heat. Pour in the egg mixture. Mixture should set immediately at edges. As eggs set, push cooked portions toward the center, letting uncooked eggs flow underneath. When the eggs are thickened and no liquid egg remains, spoon green onion and asparagus on one side. Fold the omelet in half; serve in tortilla.

I'M STUFFED FRENCH TOAST

I was able to re-create a dish I had first enjoyed while eating out. The fruit adds a delightful touch to stuffed French toast.

—**MELISSA KERRICK** AUBURN, NY

PREP: 30 MIN. • **COOK:** 5 MIN.
MAKES: 4 SERVINGS

- 2 **medium ripe bananas, sliced**
- 2 **tablespoons brown sugar**
- 1 **teaspoon banana or vanilla extract**
- 8 **ounces reduced-fat cream cheese**
- 8 **slices oat bread (½ inch thick)**
- 2 **large eggs**
- ⅔ **cup evaporated milk**
- 1¼ **teaspoons ground cinnamon**
- 1¼ **teaspoons vanilla extract**
- 1 **tablespoon butter**
- 1 **cup sliced fresh strawberries or frozen unsweetened sliced strawberries, thawed**
- ½ **cup fresh blueberries or frozen unsweetened blueberries**
- 1 **tablespoon sugar**
 Confectioners' sugar

1. In a large skillet coated with cooking spray, saute bananas with brown sugar. Stir in banana extract. In a small bowl, beat cream cheese until smooth. Add banana mixture; beat well. Spread on four slices of bread; top with remaining bread.
2. In a shallow bowl, whisk the eggs, milk, cinnamon and vanilla. Dip both sides of sandwiches in egg mixture.
3. In a large skillet, toast sandwiches in butter for 2-3 minutes on each side or until golden brown.
4. Meanwhile, in a small saucepan, combine the strawberries, blueberries and sugar; heat through. Serve with the French toast; sprinkle with the confectioners' sugar.

SAUERKRAUT LATKES

You might be skeptical of sauerkraut in potato pancakes, but it adds a lovely tang to offset the apples' sweetness.

—**AYSHA SCHURMAN** AMMON, ID

PREP: 20 MIN. • **COOK:** 5 MIN./BATCH
MAKES: 2½ DOZEN

- 3 **pounds russet potatoes, peeled and shredded**
- 1½ **cups shredded peeled apples**
- 1½ **cups sauerkraut, rinsed and well drained**
- 6 **large eggs, lightly beaten**
- 6 **tablespoons all-purpose flour**
- 2 **teaspoons salt**
- 1½ **teaspoons pepper**
- ¾ **cup canola oil**
 Sour cream and chopped green onions, optional

1. In a large bowl, combine potatoes, apples, sauerkraut and eggs. Combine the flour, salt and pepper; stir into the potato mixture.
2. Heat 2 tablespoons oil in a large nonstick skillet over medium heat. Drop batter by ¼ cupfuls into oil; press lightly to flatten. Fry in batches until golden brown on both sides, using remaining oil as needed. Drain on paper towels. Top with sour cream and green onions if desired.

ASPARAGUS OMELET TORTILLA WRAP

MASCARPONE-MUSHROOM
FRITTATA STACK

DAD'S BLUEBERRY BUTTERMILK PANCAKES

My dad makes blueberry pancakes for us every Saturday without fail. Cornmeal, oats and buttermilk give the batter a heartiness we can't resist.

—GABRIELLE SHORT PLEASANT HILL, IA

PREP: 15 MIN. + STANDING
COOK: 10 MIN./BATCH
MAKES: 12 PANCAKES

- 1 cup all-purpose flour
- 3 tablespoons cornmeal
- 3 tablespoons quick-cooking oats
- 3 tablespoons sugar
- 1 teaspoon baking powder
- ½ teaspoon baking soda
- ½ teaspoon salt
  Dash ground nutmeg
- 1 large egg
- 1½ cups buttermilk
- 2 tablespoons canola oil
- 1 teaspoon vanilla extract
- 1 cup fresh or frozen blueberries

1. In a large bowl, whisk the first eight ingredients. In another bowl, whisk egg, buttermilk, oil and vanilla until blended. Add to the flour mixture; stir just until moistened (the batter will be lumpy). Let stand 15 minutes.
2. Lightly grease a large nonstick skillet or griddle; heat over medium heat. Stir blueberries into the batter. Pour batter by ¼ cupfuls onto skillet or griddle. Cook until bubbles on top begin to pop and bottoms are golden brown. Turn; cook until the second side is brown.

MAKE IT SIZZLE

My husband prepares Saturday morning breakfast, so I stir up pancake batter and freeze it in quart-size freezer bags ahead of time. I thaw a bag in the refrigerator on Friday night. The next day, he simply clips a corner off the bag and pours the batter onto a hot skillet. This method simplifies cleanup, too.

—CHRISTI G. TULSA, OK

MASCARPONE-MUSHROOM FRITTATA STACK

When I bring this delicious egg dish to the table, get lots of accolades. It looks impressive and like it took a lot of effort but it's quite easy to prepare.

—GILDA LESTER MILLSBORO, DE

PREP: 25 MIN. • **COOK:** 20 MIN.
MAKES: 6 SERVINGS

- 8 large eggs
- ⅓ cup heavy whipping cream
- ½ cup grated Romano cheese, divided
- 1½ teaspoons salt, divided
- 5 tablespoons olive oil, divided
- ¾ pound sliced fresh mushrooms
- 1 medium onion, halved and thinly sliced
- 2 tablespoons minced fresh basil
- 2 garlic cloves, minced
- ⅛ teaspoon pepper
- 1 carton (8 ounces) mascarpone cheese

1. In a large bowl, whisk the eggs, cream, ¼ cup Romano cheese and 1 teaspoon salt.
2. In a 10-in. skillet, heat 2 tablespoons oil over medium-high heat. Add mushrooms and onion; cook and stir until tender. Add the basil, garlic, pepper and remaining salt; cook and stir 1 minute longer. Transfer mixture to a bowl; stir in mascarpone cheese and remaining Romano cheese.
3. In the same pan, heat 1 tablespoon oil over medium-high heat. Pour in ⅔ cup egg mixture. Mixture should set immediately at edges. As eggs set, push cooked portions toward the center, letting uncooked eggs flow underneath.
4. Let stand, covered, 5-7 minutes or until completely set. Remove to a serving platter; cover and keep warm. Repeat with remaining egg mixture making two additional fritattas, using remaining oil as needed.
5. Place one frittata on a serving platter; layer with half of mushroom mixture. Repeat layers. Top with remaining frittata. Cut into wedges.

SUMMER BREAKFAST SKILLET

Sizzle up spicy chorizo, veggies and eggs for a breakfast that keeps you going. If I want something easy to take on the road, I turn it into handheld tacos.

—ANDREA RIVERA WESTBURY, NY

PREP: 20 MIN. • **COOK:** 15 MIN.
MAKES: 4 SERVINGS

- ½ pound fresh chorizo or bulk spicy pork sausage
- 1 medium sweet yellow pepper, chopped
- 1 medium sweet red pepper, chopped
- 1 medium onion, chopped
- 3 medium tomatoes, chopped
- 2 small zucchini, chopped
- 2 garlic cloves, minced
- 1 teaspoon paprika
- 4 large eggs
- ¼ teaspoon salt
- ¼ teaspoon pepper
- ½ cup shredded cheddar cheese

1. In a large skillet, cook chorizo, peppers and onion over medium heat 4-6 minutes or until chorizo is cooked through, breaking the chorizo into crumbles; drain. Stir in tomatoes, zucchini, garlic and paprika; cook, covered, 5-7 minutes longer or until vegetables are tender.

2. With back of spoon, make four wells in vegetable mixture; break an egg into each well. Sprinkle the eggs with salt and pepper. Cook, covered, 4-6 minutes or until egg whites are completely set and yolks begin to thicken but are not hard.

3. Remove from heat; sprinkle with cheese. Let stand, covered, 5 minutes or until cheese is melted.

DAD'S BLUEBERRY BUTTERMILK PANCAKES

SUMMER BREAKFAST SKILLET

SKILLET BLUEBERRY
SLUMP, PAGE 98

98

96

94

DESSERTS

Dessert in a skillet? It's not only possible—it's **amazingly tasty!** Once the main meal is over, fire up the stovetop once more for a **perfect finale.** Sure, these recipes are easy to whip up, but they're also impressive.

CHOCOLATE-HAZELNUT BANANA CREPES

CHOCOLATE-HAZELNUT BANANA CREPES

Enjoy this wonderfully rich and delicious treat: warm bananas and Nutella stuffed into light and luscious homemade crepes.

—**CATHY HALL** LYNDHURST, VA

PREP: 15 MIN. + CHILLING • **COOK:** 15 MIN.
MAKES: 10 SERVINGS

- 2 **large eggs**
- 2 **large egg whites**
- ¾ **cup water**
- ½ **cup 2% milk**
- 1 **tablespoon canola oil**
- 1 **cup all-purpose flour**
- 1 **tablespoon sugar**
- ½ **teaspoon salt**
- 2 **tablespoons butter**
- 2 **tablespoons brown sugar**
- 4 **medium bananas, peeled and sliced**
- ⅓ **cup Nutella**

1. In a large bowl, whisk the eggs, egg whites, water, milk and oil. Combine the flour, sugar and salt; add to egg mixture and mix well. Refrigerate for 1 hour.

2. Heat a lightly greased 8-in. nonstick skillet over medium heat; pour ¼ cup batter into center of skillet. Lift and tilt pan to coat bottom evenly. Cook until top appears dry; turn and cook 15-20 seconds longer. Remove to a wire rack. Repeat with remaining batter, greasing skillet as needed. When cool, stack the crepes separated by waxed paper or paper towels in between.

3. In a large skillet, melt butter over medium-low heat. Stir in brown sugar until blended. Add bananas; cook for 2-3 minutes or until the bananas are glazed and slightly softened, stirring gently. Remove from the heat.

4. Spread Nutella over each crepe; top with bananas. Roll up and serve.

CARAMEL-PECAN APPLE SLICES

DESSERTS

CARAMEL-PECAN APPLE SLICES

⑤ INGREDIENTS FAST FIX

Here's a warm, decadent dessert. Ready to eat in only 15 minutes, the apples are also good alongside a pork entree or spooned over vanilla ice cream.

—**CAROL GILLESPIE** CHAMBERSBURG, PA

START TO FINISH: 15 MIN.
MAKES: 6 SERVINGS

- ⅓ cup packed brown sugar
- 2 tablespoons butter
- 2 large apples, cut into ½-inch slices
- ¼ cup chopped pecans, toasted

In a large skillet, cook and stir brown sugar and butter over medium heat until sugar is dissolved. Add the apples; cook, uncovered, over medium heat for 5-7 minutes or until tender, stirring occasionally. Stir in pecans. Serve warm.

NOTE *To toast nuts, bake in a shallow pan in a 350° oven for 5-10 minutes or cook in a skillet over low heat until lightly browned, stirring occasionally.*

CARAMEL-APPLE SKILLET BUCKLE

CHOCOLATE CINNAMON TOAST

⑤ INGREDIENTS FAST FIX

You might want to sit down for this one. Cinnamon bread gets toasted in a skillet, topped with chocolate and covered with fresh berries. That's real love.

—**JEANNE AMBROSE** MILWAUKEE, WI

START TO FINISH: 10 MIN.
MAKES: 1 SERVING

- 1 slice cinnamon bread
- 1 teaspoon butter, softened
- 2 tablespoons 60% cacao bittersweet chocolate baking chips
  Sliced banana and strawberries, optional

Spread both sides of the bread with butter. In a small skillet, toast bread over medium-high heat 2-3 minutes on each side, topping with chocolate chips after turning. Remove from the heat; spread melted chocolate evenly over toast. If desired, top with fruit.

CARAMEL-APPLE SKILLET BUCKLE

My grandma used to make a version of this for me when I was a little girl. She would use fresh apples from the tree in her backyard. I've adapted her recipe because I love the mix of apple, pecans and caramel.

—**EMILY HOBBS** SPRINGFIELD, MO

PREP: 35 MIN. • **BAKE:** 1 HOUR + STANDING
MAKES: 12 SERVINGS

- ½ cup butter, softened
- ¾ cup sugar
- 2 large eggs
- 1 teaspoon vanilla extract
- 2 cups all-purpose flour
- 2½ teaspoons baking powder
- 1¾ teaspoons ground cinnamon
- ½ teaspoon ground ginger
- ¼ teaspoon salt
- 1½ cups buttermilk

TOPPING

- ⅔ cup packed brown sugar
- ½ cup all-purpose flour
- ¼ cup cold butter
- ¾ cup finely chopped pecans
- ½ cup old-fashioned oats

- 6 cups thinly sliced peeled Gala or other sweet apples (about 6 medium)
- 18 caramels, unwrapped
- 1 tablespoon buttermilk
  Vanilla ice cream, optional

1. Preheat oven to 350°. In a large bowl, cream the butter and sugar until light and fluffy. Add the eggs, one at a time, beating well after each addition. Beat in vanilla. In another bowl, whisk the flour, baking powder, cinnamon, ginger and salt; add to creamed mixture alternately with buttermilk, beating well after each addition. Pour into a greased 12-in. ovenproof skillet.

2. For topping, in a small bowl, mix brown sugar and flour; cut in butter until crumbly. Stir in pecans and oats; sprinkle over batter. Top with apples. Bake 60-70 minutes or until apples are golden brown. Cool in the pan on a wire rack.

3. In a microwave, melt caramels with buttermilk; stir until smooth. Drizzle over cake. Let stand until set. If desired, serve with ice cream.

CRAN-APPLE COBBLER

My cranberry-packed cobbler is the crowning glory of many of our late fall and winter meals. Since my family isn't big on pies, they prefer this favorite at Thanksgiving and Christmas celebrations. The aroma of cinnamon and fruit is irresistible as it bakes.

—JO ANN SHEEHAN RUTHER GLEN, VA

PREP: 20 MIN. • **BAKE:** 30 MIN.
MAKES: 6-8 SERVINGS

- 2½ cups sliced peeled apples
- 2½ cups sliced peeled firm pears
- 1 to 1¼ cups sugar
- 1 cup fresh or frozen cranberries, thawed
- ½ cup water
- 3 tablespoons quick-cooking tapioca
- 3 tablespoons Red Hots
- ½ teaspoon ground cinnamon
- 2 tablespoons butter

TOPPING
- ¾ cup all-purpose flour
- 2 tablespoons sugar
- 1 teaspoon baking powder
- ¼ teaspoon salt
- ¼ cup cold butter, cubed
- 3 tablespoons milk
  Vanilla ice cream

1. In a large, ovenproof skillet, combine the first eight ingredients; let stand for 5 minutes. Cook and stir over medium heat until the mixture comes to a full rolling boil, about 18 minutes. Dot with butter.
2. In a small bowl, combine the flour, sugar, baking powder and salt. Cut in the butter until the mixture resembles coarse crumbs. Stir in milk until a soft dough forms.
3. Drop the topping by heaping tablespoons onto hot fruit. Bake at 375° for 30-35 minutes or until golden brown. Serve warm with ice cream.

RED VELVET CREPE CAKES

It's well worth the time to make this absolutely stunning cake. Each thin layer is separated by a rich and creamy filling. Treat your family on special occasions with this cake.

—CRYSTAL HEATON ALTON, UT

PREP: 1¼ HOURS • **COOK:** 25 MIN.
MAKES: 2 CREPE CAKES (8 SERVINGS EACH)

- 1 package red velvet cake mix (regular size)
- 2¾ cups whole milk
- 1 cup all-purpose flour
- 3 large eggs
- 3 large egg yolks
- ¼ cup butter, melted
- 3 teaspoons vanilla extract

FROSTING
- 2 packages (8 ounces each) cream cheese, softened
- 1¼ cups butter, softened
- ½ teaspoon salt
- 12 cups confectioners' sugar
- 5 teaspoons vanilla extract
  Fresh blueberries

1. In a large bowl, combine the cake mix, milk, flour, eggs, egg yolks, butter and vanilla; beat on low speed for 30 seconds. Beat on medium for 2 minutes.
2. Heat a lightly greased 8-in. nonstick skillet over medium heat; pour ¼ cup batter into center of skillet. Lift and tilt pan to coat bottom evenly. Cook until the top appears dry; turn and cook 15-20 seconds longer. Remove to a wire rack. Repeat with remaining batter, greasing skillet as needed. When cool, stack the crepes separated with waxed paper or paper towels in between.
3. For frosting, in a large bowl, beat the cream cheese, butter and salt until fluffy. Add confectioners' sugar and vanilla; beat until smooth.
4. To assemble two crepe cakes, place one crepe on each of two cake plates. Spread each with one rounded tablespoon frosting to within ½ in. of edges. Repeat layers until all crepes are used. Spread remaining frosting over tops and sides of the crepe cakes. Garnish with blueberries.

FAST FIX ▶
SAUCY SPICED PEARS

We serve these tangy, saucy pears over angel food cake, pound cake or with a little yogurt or vanilla ice cream. Sprinkle with a favorite topping.

—JOY ZACHARIA CLEARWATER, FL

START TO FINISH: 20 MIN.
MAKES: 4 SERVINGS

- ½ cup orange juice
- 2 tablespoons butter
- 2 tablespoons sugar
- 2 teaspoons lemon juice
- 1 teaspoon vanilla extract
- 1 teaspoon ground ginger
- ¼ teaspoon ground cinnamon
- ⅛ teaspoon salt
- ⅛ teaspoon ground allspice
- ⅛ teaspoon cayenne pepper, optional
- 3 large Bosc pears (about 1¾ pounds), cored, peeled and sliced
  Thinly sliced fresh mint leaves, optional

1. In a large skillet, combine the first nine ingredients and, if desired, the cayenne. Cook over medium-high heat 1-2 minutes or until butter is melted, stirring occasionally.
2. Add pears; bring to a boil. Reduce heat to medium; cook, uncovered, 3-4 minutes or until sauce is slightly thickened and pears are crisp-tender, stirring occasionally. Cool slightly. If desired, top with mint.

DID YOU KNOW?

While there are many varieties of pears, the Saucy Spiced Pears recipe specifically calls for Bosc pears because they're ideal for cooking.

BANANA SKILLET UPSIDE-DOWN CAKE

My grandmother gave me my first cast-iron skillet, and I've been cooking and baking with it ever since. Sometimes I add drained maraschino cherries to the banana skillet dessert and serve the cake with ice cream.

—**TERRI MERRITTS** NASHVILLE, TN

PREP: 25 MIN. • **BAKE:** 35 MIN.
MAKES: 10 SERVINGS

- 1 **package (14 ounces) banana quick bread and muffin mix**
- ½ **cup chopped walnuts**
- ¼ **cup butter, cubed**
- ¾ **cup packed brown sugar**
- 2 **tablespoons lemon juice**
- 4 **medium bananas, cut into ¼-inch slices**
- 2 **cups flaked coconut**

1. Preheat oven to 375°. Prepare banana bread batter according to package directions; stir in walnuts.
2. In a 10-in. ovenproof skillet, melt butter over medium heat; stir in the brown sugar until dissolved. Add lemon juice; cook and stir 2-3 minutes longer or until slightly thickened. Remove from heat. Arrange bananas in a single layer over the brown sugar mixture; sprinkle with coconut.
3. Spoon the prepared batter over coconut. Bake 35-40 minutes or until dark golden and a toothpick inserted in the center comes out clean. Cool for 5 minutes before inverting onto a serving plate. Serve warm.

**BANANA SKILLET
UPSIDE-DOWN CAKE**

CORNMEAL TOWERS
WITH STRAWBERRIES
& CREAM

SKILLET BLUEBERRY
SLUMP

CORNMEAL TOWERS WITH STRAWBERRIES & CREAM

My kids love to help make these towers. They measure, mix, whisk and build stacks. It's a family tradition and a sweet summer dessert.

—JOSIE SHAPIRO SAN FRANCISCO, CA

PREP: 40 MIN. • **COOK:** 5 MIN./BATCH
MAKES: 12 SERVINGS

- 3 **large egg whites**
- 1 **cup heavy whipping cream**
- 1 **cup cornmeal**
- 1 **cup all-purpose flour**
- 1½ **teaspoons baking powder**
- ½ **teaspoon ground cardamom**
- ¼ **teaspoon salt**
- 1¼ **cups 2% milk**
- 1 **cup whole-milk ricotta cheese**
- ¼ **cup orange juice**
- 2 **tablespoons honey**
- 1 **teaspoon almond extract**
- 1 **to 2 tablespoons butter**
- 1 **pound fresh strawberries, sliced**
- 2 **tablespoons sugar**

1. Place egg whites in a small bowl; let stand at room temperature 30 minutes. Meanwhile, in a small bowl, beat cream until soft peaks form; refrigerate, covered, until serving.

2. In a large bowl, whisk cornmeal, flour, baking powder, cardamom and salt. In another bowl, mix the milk, ricotta cheese, orange juice, honey and extract until blended. Add to the cornmeal mixture; stir just until moistened. With clean beaters, beat egg whites on high speed until stiff but not dry; fold into batter.

3. Heat a large nonstick skillet or griddle over medium heat; grease with butter. Filling a ¼-cup measure halfway with batter, pour batter onto griddle or skillet. Cook until edges begin to dry and bottoms are golden brown. Turn; cook until second side is golden brown. Cool pancakes slightly.

4. In a bowl, toss strawberries with sugar. For each serving, stack three pancakes, layering each pancake with strawberries and whipped cream.

SKILLET BLUEBERRY SLUMP

My mother-in-law made a slump of wild blueberries with dumplings and served it warm with a pitcher of farm cream. We've been eating slump for nearly 60 years!

—ELEANORE EBELING BREWSTER, MN

PREP: 25 MIN. • **BAKE:** 20 MIN.
MAKES: 6 SERVINGS

- 4 **cups fresh or frozen blueberries**
- ½ **cup sugar**
- ½ **cup water**
- 1 **teaspoon grated lemon peel**
- 1 **tablespoon lemon juice**
- 1 **cup all-purpose flour**
- 2 **tablespoons sugar**
- 2 **teaspoons baking powder**
- ½ **teaspoon salt**
- 1 **tablespoon butter**
- ½ **cup 2% milk**
  Vanilla ice cream

1. Preheat oven to 400°. In a 10-in. ovenproof skillet, combine the first five ingredients; bring to a boil. Reduce the heat; simmer, uncovered, 9-11 minutes or until slightly thickened, stirring occasionally.

2. Meanwhile, in a small bowl, whisk flour, sugar, baking powder and salt. Cut in butter until mixture resembles coarse crumbs. Add milk; stir just until moistened.

3. Drop batter in six portions on top of the simmering blueberry mixture. Transfer to oven. Bake, uncovered, 17-20 minutes or until the dumplings are golden brown. Serve warm with ice cream.

PLUM UPSIDE-DOWN CAKE

The delicate flavor of plums is a pleasing change of pace in this upside-down cake.

—**BOBBIE TALBOTT** VENETA, OR

PREP: 15 MIN. • **BAKE:** 40 MIN.
MAKES: 8-10 SERVINGS

- ⅓ cup butter
- ½ cup packed brown sugar
- 2 pounds fresh plums, pitted and halved
- 2 large eggs
- ⅔ cup sugar
- 1 cup all-purpose flour
- 1 teaspoon baking powder
- ¼ teaspoon salt
- ⅓ cup hot water
- ½ teaspoon lemon extract
  Whipped cream, optional

1. Melt butter in a 10-in. cast-iron or ovenproof skillet. Sprinkle brown sugar over butter. Arrange the plum halves, cut side down, in a single layer over sugar; set aside.

2. In a large bowl, beat eggs until thick and lemon-colored; gradually beat in sugar. Combine the flour, baking powder and salt; add to egg mixture and mix well. Blend water and lemon extract; beat into batter. Pour over plums.

3. Bake at 350° for 40-45 minutes or until a toothpick inserted near the center comes out clean. Immediately invert onto a serving plate. Serve warm with whipped cream if desired.

CINNAMON-SUGAR APPLE PIE

Apple pie baked in a cast-iron skillet is a real stunner. This beauty, with its flaky, tender crust, also works well in a 9-inch deep-dish pie plate.

—**RENEE SCHETTLER ROSSI** NEW YORK, NY

PREP: 1 HOUR + CHILLING
BAKE: 65 MIN. + COOLING
MAKES: 10 SERVINGS

- 2½ cups all-purpose flour
- ½ teaspoon salt
- 1¼ cups cold lard
- 6 to 8 tablespoons cold 2% milk

FILLING

- 2½ cups sugar
- 1 teaspoon ground cinnamon

CINNAMON-SUGAR APPLE PIE

- ½ teaspoon ground ginger
- 9 cups thinly sliced peeled tart apples (about 9 medium)
- 1 tablespoon bourbon, optional
- 2 tablespoons all-purpose flour
  Dash salt
- 3 tablespoons cold butter, cubed

TOPPING

- 1 tablespoon 2% milk
- 2 teaspoons coarse sugar

1. In a large bowl, mix flour and salt; cut in lard until crumbly. Gradually add milk, tossing with a fork until dough holds together when pressed. Divide the dough in half. Shape each portion into a disk; wrap in plastic wrap. Refrigerate 1 hour or overnight.

2. For filling, in a large bowl, mix the sugar, cinnamon and ginger. Add the apples and toss to coat. Cover; let stand 1 hour to allow apples to release juices, stirring occasionally.

3. Drain apples, reserving the syrup. Place syrup and, if desired, bourbon

in a small saucepan; bring to a boil. Reduce heat; simmer, uncovered, 20-25 minutes or until the mixture thickens slightly and turns a medium amber color. Remove from heat; cool syrup completely.

4. Preheat oven to 400°. Toss drained apples with flour and salt. On a lightly floured surface, roll one half of the dough to a ⅛-in.-thick circle; transfer to a 10-in. cast-iron or other deep ovenproof skillet. Trim pastry even with rim. Add apple mixture. Pour cooled syrup over top; dot with butter.

5. Roll remaining dough to a ⅛-in.-thick circle. Place over filling. Trim, seal and flute edge. Cut slits in top. Brush milk over pastry; sprinkle with coarse sugar. Place pie on a foil-lined baking sheet. Bake 20 minutes.

6. Reduce oven setting to 350°. Bake 45-55 minutes longer or until crust is golden brown and the filling is bubbly. Cool on a wire rack.

MAKE IT SIZZLE

This recipe is great! It turned out just the way it was promised, and I followed the recipe to its entirety. This was for my niece's Thanksgiving potluck, and they confirmed its deliciousness. The only thing I added was decorative leaves. I rolled the leftover dough from trimming the edges and cut a small leaf design out. I cut a small indention down the middle to resemble the veins in the leaf and used red and yellow food coloring. It made it a little more unique and fitting for the occasion.

—**NATHANALLENDANIEL** TASTEOFHOME.COM

WALKING TACOS,
PAGE 107

104

103

102

BONUS: CAST-IRON & CAMPFIRE CLASSICS

That's right—these dishes are **ready for the open flame.** Grab your **cast-iron skillet** and fill up the cooler because dinner is in the great outdoors tonight! Packing up for your next trip has **never been easier.**

THYMED ZUCCHINI SAUTE

SKILLET NACHOS

(5) INGREDIENTS FAST FIX ▶

THYMED ZUCCHINI SAUTE

Simple and flavorful, this recipe is a tasty, healthful way to use up all those zucchini from the garden. And it's ready in no time!
—**BOBBY TAYLOR** ULSTER PARK, NY

START TO FINISH: 15 MIN.
MAKES: 4 SERVINGS

- 1 tablespoon olive oil
- 1 pound medium zucchini, quartered lengthwise and halved
- ¼ cup finely chopped onion
- ½ vegetable bouillon cube, crushed
- 2 tablespoons minced fresh parsley
- 1 teaspoon minced fresh thyme or ¼ teaspoon dried thyme

In a large cast-iron or other ovenproof skillet, heat oil over medium-high heat. Add the zucchini, onion and bouillon; cook and stir 4-5 minutes or until the zucchini is crisp-tender. Sprinkle with herbs.

NOTE *This recipe was prepared with Knorr vegetable bouillon.*

FAST FIX ▶

SKILLET NACHOS

My mom gave me a fundraiser cookbook, and the recipe I've used most is for skillet nachos. My whole family's on board. For toppings, try out sour cream, tomatoes, jalapeno and red onion.
—**JUDY HUGHES** WAVERLY, KS

START TO FINISH: 30 MIN.
MAKES: 6 SERVINGS

- 1 pound ground beef
- 1 can (14½ ounces) diced tomatoes, undrained
- 1 cup fresh or frozen corn, thawed
- ¾ cup uncooked instant rice
- ½ cup water
- 1 envelope taco seasoning
- ½ teaspoon salt
- 1 cup (4 ounces) shredded Colby-Monterey Jack cheese
- 1 package (16 ounces) tortilla chips
  Optional toppings: sour cream, sliced fresh jalapenos, shredded lettuce and lime wedges

1. In a large cast-iron or other ovenproof skillet, cook beef over medium heat 6-8 minutes or until meat is no longer pink, breaking into crumbles; drain. Stir in the tomatoes, corn, rice, water, taco seasoning and salt. Bring to a boil. Reduce the heat; simmer, covered, 8-10 minutes until the rice is tender and the mixture is slightly thickened.

2. Remove from heat; sprinkle with cheese. Let stand, covered, 5 minutes or until cheese is melted. Divide the tortilla chips among six plates; spoon beef mixture over chips. Serve with toppings as desired.

FAST FIX ▶
SAUSAGE EGG SUBS

Spicy chunks of sausage give winning flavor to this scrambled egg mixture. Served in a bun, it's a satisfying all-in-one sandwich for breakfast or lunch.
—DEE PASTERNAK BRISTOL, IN

START TO FINISH: 30 MIN.
MAKES: 6 SERVINGS

- 1¼ pounds bulk pork sausage
- ¼ cup chopped onion
- 12 large eggs, lightly beaten
- ½ cup chopped fresh mushrooms
- 1 to 2 tablespoons finely chopped green pepper
- 1 to 2 tablespoons finely chopped sweet red pepper
- 6 submarine sandwich buns (about 6 inches), split

1. In a large cast-iron or other ovenproof skillet, cook sausage and onion over medium heat until meat is no longer pink; drain. Remove with a slotted spoon and keep warm.
2. In the same skillet, over medium heat cook and stir eggs for 6-7 minutes or until nearly set. Add mushrooms, peppers and the sausage mixture. Cook until the eggs are completely set and mixture is heated through. Serve on buns.

FAST FIX ▶
PAN-FRIED VENISON STEAK

Growing up, this recipe was a family favorite when we had deer meat. I loved it, and now my children do, too!
—GAYLEEN GROTE BATTLEVIEW, ND

START TO FINISH: 25 MIN.
MAKES: 4 SERVINGS

- 1 pound venison or beef tenderloin, cut into ½-inch slices
- 2 cups crushed saltines
- 2 large eggs
- ¾ cup milk
- 1 teaspoon salt
- ½ teaspoon pepper
- 5 tablespoons canola oil

1. Flatten venison to ¼-in. thickness. Place saltines in a shallow bowl. In another shallow bowl, whisk the eggs, milk, salt and pepper. Coat venison with saltines, then dip in egg mixture and coat a second time with saltines.
2. In a large cast-iron or other ovenproof skillet over medium heat, cook the venison in oil in batches for 2-3 minutes on each side or until the meat reaches desired doneness (for medium-rare, a thermometer should read 145°; medium, 160°; well-done, 170°).

CAMPFIRE HASH

In our area we're able to camp almost all year-round. My family invented this recipe using ingredients we all love so we could enjoy them on the fire. This meal tastes so good after a full day of outdoor activities.
—JANET DANILOW WINKLEMAN, AZ

PREP: 15 MIN. • **COOK:** 40 MIN.
MAKES: 6 SERVINGS

- 1 large onion, chopped
- 2 tablespoons canola oil
- 2 garlic cloves, minced
- 4 large potatoes, peeled and cubed (about 2 pounds)
- 1 pound smoked kielbasa or Polish sausage, halved and sliced
- 1 can (4 ounces) chopped green chilies
- 1 can (15¼ ounces) whole kernel corn, drained

1. In a large cast-iron or other ovenproof skillet over medium heat, cook and stir the onion in oil under tender. Add the garlic; cook 1 minute longer. Add the potatoes. Cook the mixture, uncovered, for 20 minutes, stirring occasionally.
2. Add kielbasa; cook and stir until meat and potatoes are tender and browned, about 10-15 minutes. Stir in chilies and corn; heat through.

DID YOU KNOW?

When you notice food sticking to your cast-iron skillet, it's time for reseasoning. Here's how:
- Line the lower rack of your oven with aluminum foil and preheat the oven to 350°.
- Scrub the pan with hot, soapy water and a stiff brush to remove any rust.
- Towel-dry and apply a thin coat of vegetable oil to the entire pan—outside and handle included.
- Place on top oven rack, upside down; bake for 1 hour.
- Turn off the oven and leave the pan inside to cool. Then you're all set to cook again!

SAUSAGE EGG SUBS

BLACK BEAN AND CORN TACOS

½ teaspoon salt
¼ teaspoon pepper
1 cup (4 ounces) shredded cheddar cheese

1. In a large cast-iron or other ovenproof skillet, cook the bacon and the onion over medium heat until bacon is crisp. Drain, reserving ¼ cup drippings in pan.
2. Stir in the hash browns. Cook, uncovered, over medium heat for 10 minutes or until the bottom is golden brown; turn the potatoes. With the back of a spoon, make eight evenly spaced wells in potato mixture. Break one egg into each well. Sprinkle with salt and pepper.
3. Cook, covered, on low 10 minutes or until the eggs are set and potatoes are tender. Sprinkle with cheese; let stand until cheese is melted.

FAST FIX
SESAME DILL FISH
Crispy fillets are a snap to make. I adapted a recipe originally meant for pork into a quick-cooking fish dish.
—**LINDA HESS** CHILLIWACK, BC

START TO FINISH: 15 MIN.
MAKES: 4 SERVINGS

½ cup dry bread crumbs
¼ cup sesame seeds
½ teaspoon dill weed
¼ teaspoon salt
¾ cup plain yogurt
1 pound catfish or other whitefish fillets
¼ cup canola oil
  Lemon wedges, optional

1. In a shallow bowl, combine bread crumbs, sesame seeds, dill and salt. Place yogurt in another bowl. Dip fillets in yogurt; shake off excess, then dip in crumb mixture.
2. Heat the oil in a large cast-iron or other ovenproof skillet. Fry fillets over medium-high heat for 2-3 minutes on each side or until the fish flakes easily with a fork. Serve the fish with lemon wedges if desired.

FAST FIX
BLACK BEAN AND CORN TACOS

We eat meatless meals a few times a week, so I replaced the beef with nutty brown rice to make these satisfying tacos. I also like to swap rice for quinoa.
—**KRISTIN RIMKUS** SNOHOMISH, WA

START TO FINISH: 30 MIN.
MAKES: 4 SERVINGS

1 medium onion, finely chopped
1 medium green pepper, finely chopped
1 small sweet red pepper, finely chopped
1 can (15 ounces) black beans, rinsed and drained
2 large tomatoes, seeded and chopped
2 cups shredded cabbage
1 cup fresh or frozen corn
2 tablespoons reduced-sodium taco seasoning
2 tablespoons lime juice
2 garlic cloves, minced
1 cup ready-to-serve brown rice
8 taco shells, warmed
½ cup shredded Mexican cheese blend
½ cup sour cream

1. In a large cast-iron or other ovenproof skillet, saute onion and peppers until crisp-tender. Add the beans, tomatoes, cabbage, corn, taco seasoning, lime juice and garlic. Cook and stir over medium heat for 8-10 minutes or until the vegetables are tender. Stir in rice; heat through.
2. Spoon the bean mixture into taco shells. Top the tacos with cheese and sour cream.

5 INGREDIENTS FAST FIX
SHEEPHERDER'S BREAKFAST
When we were camping, my sister-in-law always made this delicious breakfast dish. Serve with toast, juice and milk or coffee for a sure hit! One-dish casseroles like this are as good made in the kitchen and were a big help while I was raising nine children. Now I've passed the recipe on them.
—**PAULETTA BUSHNELL** ALBANY, OR

START TO FINISH: 30 MIN.
MAKES: 8 SERVINGS

¾ pound bacon strips, finely chopped
1 medium onion, chopped
1 package (30 ounces) frozen shredded hash brown potatoes, thawed
8 large eggs

MANGO CHUTNEY CHICKEN CURRY

My father came up with this curry and chutney dish. Now my family cooks it on all our road trips—in rain and sun, in the mountains, even on the beach. Adjust the curry for taste and heat.

—DINA MORENO SEATTLE, WA

START TO FINISH: 25 MIN.
MAKES: 4 SERVINGS

- 1 **tablespoon canola oil**
- 1 **pound boneless skinless chicken breasts, cubed**
- 1 **tablespoon curry powder**
- 2 **garlic cloves, minced**
- ¼ **teaspoon salt**
- ¼ **teaspoon pepper**
- ½ **cup mango chutney**
- ½ **cup half-and-half cream**

1. In a large cast-iron or other ovenproof skillet, heat the oil over medium-high heat; brown chicken. Stir in curry powder, garlic, salt and pepper; cook 1-2 minutes longer or until aromatic.

2. Stir in chutney and cream. Bring to boil. Reduce heat; simmer, uncovered, 4-6 minutes or until the chicken is no longer pink, stirring occasionally.

**MANGO CHUTNEY
CHICKEN CURRY**

SKILLET POTATO MEDLEY

SKILLET POTATO MEDLEY

The pretty potatoes I had just harvested from my garden inspired me to mix them up for dinner. The results: a wonderful, colorful side dish.

—**LORI MERRICK** DANVERS, IL

PREP: 25 MIN. • **COOK:** 15 MIN.
MAKES: 8 SERVINGS

- 2 **medium Yukon Gold potatoes (about ¾ pound)**
- 2 **medium red potatoes (about ¾ pound)**
- 2 **small purple potatoes (about ½ pound)**
- 5 **tablespoons butter**
- 1 **tablespoon olive oil**
- 1 **large sweet potato (about 1 pound)**
- 1 **cup chopped sweet onion**
- 1 **teaspoon garlic salt**
- ¼ **teaspoon dried rosemary, crushed**
- ¼ **teaspoon dried thyme**
- ¼ **teaspoon pepper**

1. Cut Yukon Gold, red and purple potatoes into ¼-in. cubes. In a large cast-iron or other ovenproof skillet, heat the butter and oil over medium heat. Add cubed potatoes; cook and stir 5 minutes.

2. Peel and cut sweet potato into ¼-in. cubes; add to skillet. Add the remaining ingredients; cook and stir 10-12 minutes or until the potatoes are tender.

WALKING TACOS

WALKING TACOS

Walking Tacos are great for an on-the-go or campfire dinner. Put all the ingredients right into the chip bags!

—**BEVERLY MATTHEWS** PASCO, WA

PREP: 10 MIN. • **COOK:** 30 MIN.
MAKES: 5 SERVINGS

- 1 **pound ground beef**
- 1 **envelope reduced-sodium chili seasoning mix**
- ¼ **teaspoon pepper**
- 1 **can (10 ounces) diced tomatoes and green chilies**
- 1 **can (15 ounces) Ranch Style beans (pinto beans in seasoned tomato sauce)**
- 5 **packages (1 ounce each) corn chips**
  Toppings: shredded cheddar cheese, sour cream and sliced green onions

1. In a large cast-iron or other ovenproof skillet, cook beef over medium heat 6-8 minutes or until no longer pink, breaking into crumbles; drain. Stir in chili seasoning mix, pepper, tomatoes and beans; bring to a boil. Reduce the heat; simmer mixture, uncovered, 20-25 minutes or until thickened, stirring occasionally.
2. Just before serving, cut open corn chip bags. Add the beef mixture and toppings as desired.

MAKE IT SIZZLE

The recipe was great—it was a hit at my parents' house because we made them and sat outside around the fire with all our guests who loved them! We made margaritas and had a blast! Thank you for the GREAT idea and recipe!

—**MARYEW17** TASTEOFHOME.COM

FLUFFY SCRAMBLED EGGS

⑤ INGREDIENTS **FAST FIX**

FLUFFY SCRAMBLED EGGS

When our son wants something heftier than cold cereal in the morning, he whips up these eggs. They're easy to make when you're camping, too. Cheese sauce and evaporated milk make them extra creamy.

—**CHRIS PFLEGHAAR** ELK RIVER, MN

START TO FINISH: 15 MIN.
MAKES: 3 SERVINGS

- 6 **large eggs**
- ¼ **cup evaporated milk or half-and-half cream**
- ¼ **teaspoon salt**
- ⅛ **teaspoon pepper**
- 1 **tablespoon canola oil**
- 2 **tablespoons process cheese sauce**

In a bowl, whisk the eggs, milk, salt and pepper. In a large cast-iron or other ovenproof skillet, heat oil over medium heat. Pour in egg mixture; stir in cheese sauce. Cook and stir until eggs are thickened and no liquid egg remains.

⑤ INGREDIENTS

CAMPFIRE FRIED FISH

This classic recipe will have lunch ready in no time. Feel free to modify by frying up any fish you've caught.

—**TASTE OF HOME** TEST KITCHEN

PREP: 15 MIN. • **COOK:** 10 MIN./BATCH
MAKES: 6 SERVINGS

- 2 **large eggs**
- ¾ **cup all-purpose flour**
- ½ **cup cornmeal**
- 1 **teaspoon salt**
- 1 **teaspoon paprika**
- 3 **pounds walleye, bluegill or perch fillets**
  Canola oil

1. In a shallow bowl, whisk eggs. In a large resealable plastic bag, combine the flour, cornmeal, salt and paprika. Dip fillets in the eggs, then roll in the flour mixture.
2. Add ¼ in. of oil to a large cast-iron skillet; place skillet on grill rack over medium-hot heat. Fry fillets in oil in batches for 3-4 minutes on each side or until fish flakes easily with a fork.

GENERAL INDEX

ALPHABETICAL INDEX